TCHEKOV at the HOUSE of SPECIAL PURPOSE

R. Johns

With reference to Chekhov's Three Sisters

CURRENCY PRESS
The performing arts publisher

CURRENT THEATRE SERIES

First published in 2019
by Currency Press Pty Ltd,
PO Box 2287, Strawberry Hills, NSW, 2012, Australia
enquiries@currency.com.au
www.currency.com.au

in association with La Mama Theatre, Melbourne

Copyright: *Tchekov At the House of Special Purpose* © R. Johns, 2017, 2019.

COPYING FOR EDUCATIONAL PURPOSES
The Australian *Copyright Act 1968* (Act) allows a maximum of one chapter or 10% of this book, whichever is the greater, to be copied by any educational institution for its educational purposes provided that that educational institution (or the body that administers it) has given a remuneration notice to Copyright Agency (CA) under the Act.
For details of the CA licence for educational institutions contact CA, 11/66 Goulburn Street, Sydney, NSW, 2000; tel: within Australia 1800 066 844 toll free; outside Australia 61 2 9394 7600; fax: 61 2 9394 7601; email: info@copyright.com.au

COPYING FOR OTHER PURPOSES
Except as permitted under the Act, for example a fair dealing for the purposes of study, research, criticism or review, no part of this book may be reproduced, stored in a retrieval system, or transmitted in any form or by any means without prior written permission. All enquiries should be made to the publisher at the address above.

Any performance or public reading of *Tchekov At the House of Special Purpose* is forbidden unless a licence has been received from the author or the author's agent. The purchase of this book in no way gives the purchaser the right to perform the play in public, whether by means of a staged production or a reading. All applications for public performance should be addressed to the author c/- Currency Press.

Typeset by Dean Nottle for Currency Press.
Cover design: Peter Mumford in homage to Lazar Markovich Lissitzky 'Beat the Whites with the Red Wedge'.

Currency Press acknowledges the Traditional Owners of the Country on which we live and work. We pay our respects to all Aboriginal and Torres Strait Islander Elders, past and present.

A catalogue record for this book is available from the National Library of Australia

Contents

TCHEKOV AT THE HOUSE OF SPECIAL PURPOSE

Act One	1
Act Two	25
Act Three	40
Act Four	51

Theatre Program at the end of the playtext

This script is dedicated to Peter Stratford, my mentor, and dear friend who was always willing to advise, inspire, read drafts as every character, and ask, 'Who, what, where and why?' A wonderfully brave actor, with a voice of honey, his final performance was as Doctor Botkin in Tchekov at the House of Special Purpose. I miss him so much, always playful, curious and insightful. We had so many adventures together. Even at eighty, he had the heart of youth.

Photo: Laura Owsianka

Tchekov At the House of Special Purpose was first presented at La Mama Courthouse Theatre, Melbourne, on 25 October, 2017 with the following cast:

MARIA	Yvette Turner
ANASTASIA	Asleen Mauthoor
TATIANA	Meg Turner
OLGA	Alice Batt
ALEXANDRA	Carolyn Bock
CITIZEN NICHOLAS	Jim Daly
DR EUGENY BOTKIN	Peter Stratford
KHARITONOV	Gregory. J. Fryer
OXANA	Milijana Čančar
GUARD	Maria Paula Afanador
YUROVSKY	Adam May
IVAN	Huw Jennings

Director, Alex Menglet
Production Design, Peter Mumford
Lighting Design, Shane Grant,
Sound Design and Stage Management, Millie Levakis-Lucas

CHARACTERS

THE PRISONERS

>MARIA, 19, the least aristocratic of the sisters, and the most adventurous, the one who feels more than her sisters, and who yearns too much.
>
>ANASTASIA, 17, has the enthusiasm of youth, exuberant, self-centered and charming. Longs to be an actress.
>
>TATIANA, 21, of all the sisters, she is the Grand Duchess in training to be Empress, knows how to use her elegance and her intelligence.
>
>OLGA, 22, degree of suffering post-traumatic stress.
>
>ALEXANDRA, 46, imperious. Passionate about Nicky, but would never expose her emotions before the common horde. Iron-willed yet addicted to pills.
>
>CITIZEN NICHOLAS, 50, worn and weary. He never wanted to be Tsar. He is a man whose duty has circumscribed his life. The most unassuming of the royals, even if he expects respect. He realises too late that he has lost control to others.
>
>ALEXEI, the young sick son of Nicholas and Alexandra. The violin is played offstage by Alexei. It becomes his voice, as he is never seen. It is the playing of a learner.
>(The violin playing is also often linked to Alexandra, at times on stage or exiting. She is the one who appreciates it, whilst Oxana and her guards wince at it.)

THE RETAINERS

>DR EUGENY BOTKIN, 53, a gentle man who has given up too much for duty. Sick and in a wheelchair.
>
>KHARITONOV, 46, the chef. Incredibly proud of his abilities as a chef to the Tsar. He feels he has the duty to work in reduced circumstances and keep up appearances. He is soft like dough. He takes Olga under his wing and has the inner belief if only we all could eat there would be no war.

THE GUARDS

OXANA, second-in-command to Commissar Avadeyev in charge of the house. She has changed sides, from chamber maid to Bolshevik. She has the power of life and death over the aristocrats. However, she finds it difficult to know how to deal with this royal family and her frustration emerges like a scream from Gogol in the second act.

GUARD, never named. Seemingly obsessive about protocols, but in reality far more interested in power than ideology or people. Constantly noting down what people say.

YUROVSKY, 40, a member of the secret police, precise and sharp. Dissembling and intelligent. He is the perfect servant for ideology. He remembers the oppression he and his family have suffered.

IVAN, 18, a naïve guard. He is swept up in the revolution, follows the philosophy that life will become better. Smitten by the gorgeous girl Maria who seems to like him.

SETTING

A room in a provincial house, 'The House of Special Purpose', Ekaterinburg, 1918. The production takes us into a poetic space, the room is full of suitcases and packing cases, where life is in transit.

A NOTE ON THE TEXT

In this new take on a Chekhov play, *Three Sisters*, the family of the plot has changed to that of the once Tsar, now 'Citizen' Nicholas. Family and retainers are imprisoned in the provincial 'House of Special Purpose', watched day and night by Bolshevik guards.

It is a fact the Romanov girls performed Chekhov to pass the time under house arrest.

But what happens in this last house of existential chaos, youth versus age, hope versus paranoia, and love versus fear, where some guards are as confused about the end point of their surveillance as the Romanovs are about their imprisonment?

The play is not intended as documentary nor ethnography, it is a heightened, immersive experience that focusses on how we retain our humanity amidst revolution.

This play went to press before the end of rehearsals and may differ from the play as performed.

ACT ONE

SCENE ONE

The set is made up of scattered suitcases. Packing cases at the back create a wall above head height. Three tea chests high in the middle, lower on the sides, with an entrance through the middle for the prisoners. Suggesting that life is in transit, nothing is permanent.

Seats are the packing case centre back, the packing case stage left, and the packing case stage right. Downstage a packing case will be revealed, at the end of Act Three, as a bath, when the lid is opened. A chandelier hangs from the lighting bars, a reminder of another time.

The set is not dressed, only the audience sitting with blacks around them, are seemingly in a theatre.

IVAN *rushes on.*

IVAN: They're coming! They're coming!

    A GUARD *enters, writing in her notebook. She lifts her eyes, sees* IVAN.

GUARD: Hey!

    IVAN *stops dead in his tracks.*

Where is your rifle?

IVAN: Oh … oh … sorry … they're coming!

    IVAN *exits. The* GUARD *continues writing.*

GUARD: Running without rifle.

    A large vertical packing case opens and OXANA *steps out, slowly. She is tired.*

OXANA: What's all the noise? What's happening? Quiet! God, why can't I sleep? Just to sleep. Why can't I get enough sleep?! I'll fix them all! Out!

    The GUARD *and* OXANA *exit.*

As the first bars of music play, ANASTASIA, TATIANA *and* MARIA *enter from the other entrances. They dance a minuet.*

NICHOLAS *and* ALEXANDRA *enter.* NICHOLAS *stands centre stage, as the women dance in a circle.*

There is an oranges and lemons game as the minuet ends and NICHOLAS *and* ALEXANDRA *pass under the arch of the girls' raised arms. There is a mock 'Chop off your head' and everyone laughs.*

NICHOLAS *and* ALEXANDRA *sit on the front packing cases. The girls pose behind them and a photograph is taken. A puff of smoke.*

The music cuts out. NICHOLAS *exits, then* ALEXANDRA, *followed by* OLGA. ANASTASIA *calls out.*

ANASTASIA: Chekhov! We must rehearse the new play. To Moscow! To Moscow! Sisters! *Three Sisters!*

The audience are positioned as if they are the outer view from the room. There are no literal windows—they are mimed on the fourth wall.

TATIANA: But, we don't even know how long they will keep us here.
MARIA: The window!

The following dialogue is fast, each cutting across the end of the other's sentence. A sisterly fight.

TATIANA: Don't!
ANASTASIA: Can we just rehearse?
TATIANA: You could be shot.
MARIA: [*yelling*] Get us out of here!
ANASTASIA: If you explore who your character is—
MARIA: Help us!
ANASTASIA: You'll feel free.
MARIA: Out there! Over the fences!
TATIANA: They're not going to risk their lives.
MARIA: Can you see me?

The sound of a gunshot.

TATIANA: Killers who will kill you.
MARIA: Not if we hide in here!

ACT ONE

They enter one of the large 'surreal' packing-sized cases, lined with Russian newspapers, and hide inside.

The sound of another gunshot.

[*Shocked*] They shot at me. They shot at me.

With their hands, they break the newspaper that lines the packing case and burst out of it.

TATIANA: [*examining* MARIA*'s hand*] It's grazed. I warned you.

   TATIANA *winds a ribbon from her dress around* MARIA*'s hand.*

ANASTASIA: The world of the play is a better world to live in. We have to keep acting. They can't take that away from us. They can't destroy that.

   The GUARD *enters in a hurry, with* IVAN *who is carrying a rifle.*

TATIANA: He'll report us now.

   The GUARD *stares at* MARIA *and talks only to her throughout this scene.*

   IVAN *stumbles, as he reads haltingly from an instruction book.*

IVAN: Don't/ stand/ by/ the/ windows. Repeat the rule.

ANASTASIA, TATIANA *and* MARIA: [*in unison*] Don't stand by the windows. Repeat the rule.

IVAN: So why do you stand there? You must obey orders.

ANASTASIA, TATIANA *and* MARIA: [*in unison*] Obey orders.

IVAN: I am following orders, and you are not to show yourself, even if no-one sees you.

MARIA: What, to shoot at us?

IVAN: No-one out there is to see 'former' people in here.

MARIA: It was just my hand.

IVAN: That is why I fired a warning. I didn't want to hurt you.

TATIANA: You are holding us illegally. No trial.

IVAN: This is my only way to support my mother; otherwise we'd have no bread.

TATIANA: Is your mother proud of you?

ANASTASIA: Locking us up?

MARIA: How does your mother survive in this new world?

IVAN: Her hands aren't soft and white like yours.

> TATIANA *and* MARIA *step closer to* IVAN.

The new commander doesn't want any trouble.

> *As the questioning continues all the girls start to circle* IVAN, *until they surround him, usurping his power until the* GUARD *enters.*

ANASTASIA: How old is he?
IVAN: What? That's a stupid question.
ANASTASIA: We like playing guessing games to pass the time.
IVAN: Games are for the rich.
TATIANA: Is he sixty?
MARIA: Fifty?
ANASTASIA: Forty?
TATIANA: You blinked! He's forty.
ANASTASIA: Is he a learned man?
TATIANA: A man of the people?
IVAN: No.
MARIA: Does he hit his wife? You can tell us. Nothing's private anymore.

> *The* GUARD *steps forward, wearing a holster and gun.*

GUARD: Who was at that window?
MARIA: I was.
GUARD: [*to* IVAN] What were you doing, idiot? To miss your target? If you decide to shoot, make it count! You need more practice.
IVAN: [*looking at* MARIA] The sun was in my eyes.
GUARD: With the new second-in-command just arrived! There'll be hell to pay. [*To* TATIANA] You. Get the old man.

> TATIANA *exits.*

[*Sharply to* MARIA, *who sits*] Stand up.
MARIA: Today is my birthday. I am nineteen.
GUARD: Does she want a medal? This will have to be reported. What was she doing?

> IVAN *shrugs and shuffles uncomfortably.*

ANASTASIA: Rehearsing. We are going to put on a play.
GUARD: Who gave permission?
MARIA: What else is there to do?
GUARD: The directive is to do nothing.

ACT ONE

MARIA/ANASTASIA: We know.
GUARD: No. Criminals don't know anything.

She takes out a little notebook and makes notes in pencil.

DR BOTKIN *enters in his wheelchair, holding his small medical book. He is pushed through the entrance at the back by* TATIANA.

BOTKIN: When the Emperor of all Russia's hair is coming out ... dissolve quarter an ounce of mothballs in half a bottle of spirit ... Now what is wrong with your hand, princess? Not that I will be able to get any medicine.

He looks at MARIA*'s hand.*

This makes me cry. Did you think she would creep through that window? Run away?
GUARD: She is lucky to be walking in this room free.
ANASTASIA: Dear Eugeny Sergeevich!
BOTKIN: What does my other princess want?
ANASTASIA: I want to feel as if I were soaring under the broad blue sky with great white birds around me. Why is that? Why?
BOTKIN: [*to* ANASTASIA] My white bird ...

He kisses MARIA*'s hand.*

[*Gently*] ... your doctor knows, love will make it better.
MARIA: When I woke up today, I vowed everything in life would be open to me.
GUARD: Privilege is for those who work.
ANASTASIA: We went to the Moscow Art Theatre with Papa. We saw that Chekhov play. I'd work so hard if I could be an actress.
BOTKIN: [*tenderly*] Indeed, indeed.
GUARD: Make believe is sickness.
ANASTASIA: I could pretend to break stones, or work in a laundry and play the part well.
GUARD: [*to* IVAN] Get on with it! Fix it up!

IVAN *fixes the newspaper in the packing case, sealing it up again.*

IVAN: Soon none of us will work anymore. We're taking all the jewels and estates of the rich and sharing them around the poor, and then there'll be enough for everyone.

GUARD: Every rich parasite must be made to work. Every one!
ANASTASIA: When we were imprisoned at Tobolsk, the guards let Papa and us build a little theatre and we performed Tchekov's *The Bear*.
GUARD: Oh, they built a little theatre. They must have bribed those bastards.
TATIANA: If this is our room we should be able to do what we like in it.
GUARD: [*to* IVAN] Back on duty! Outside!

> MARIA *follows* IVAN *out as he exits, just as* OXANA *enters.*
>
> OXANA *avoids all eye contact with the girls until* TATIANA *names her.*

Commander Pitrienko! Welcome!
OXANA: [*fast, stopping* MARIA] Where do you think you're going?
MARIA: The walkway.
OXANA: [*fast*] Why?
MARIA: Look at how high the fences are to keep us in.
OXANA: [*fast*] The new party directive. Section 73, subsection A. Clause B. One half-hour walking the inner perimeter under supervision.
MARIA: But it's a special day.
GUARD: [*spouting party ideology*] Every special day they had, they stole from the people.
MARIA: What did we steal?
TATIANA: On birthdays thousands of candles would flicker, the jewels on all the gowns would shine as the band struck up.
OXANA: [*to the* GUARD] And with every step of the dance they oppressed someone with their superiority. The regulation is you are forbidden to talk about the former days.
TATIANA: Did you ever dance?
OXANA: No.
TATIANA: I'm sure I've met you in the past.
OXANA: Did you see my face over a bayonet?
TATIANA: You look familiar.

> *Pause as this registers with* OXANA.

OXANA: All soldiers look the same. Even the women. Gone are the lullabies I sang, once upon a time.
MARIA: Please let me go outside. I want to watch the wall being built.

ACT ONE

OXANA: There is no freedom to do what you want. Like putting your arm out of a window. Why is there dust here?

MARIA: What do you mean?

OXANA crosses down to the packing box at the front of the stage, indicating to MARIA to place her foot on it.

OXANA: I am looking at your feet, prisoner. Collecting dust. But with me you are safe, otherwise your doll's feet would be broken and thrown away.

TATIANA: [*to* ANASTASIA] Don't you cry. The doctor will always help us.

BOTKIN: I may as well be dead. I am not even allowed to read the paper. I write letters ... but what to write ... I don't know ... God only knows.

IVAN brings in a cake that looks like a brick—flat and tired.

IVAN: From the nuns, there's a cake for the prisoners. They begged us.

TATIANA: Thank you. Please thank them.

The three girls flock to take cake. OXANA *stops them, holding up her arms.*

OXANA: I like cake.

IVAN: [*louder*] Please, for the love of God, let us feed the prisoners! The nuns said.

OXANA: Cake is for those who deserve it.

She sits at the front and starts to eat. Disappointed, angry, annoyed, each with a different emotion, the girls cross back to their previous positions.

Fan!

She points to a fan in an open suitcase.

It's extremely hot.

IVAN steps forward with a fan. The GUARD *takes it off him and takes over fanning* OXANA *whilst* OXANA *almost poses like royalty.*

There should be four girls here.

TATIANA: We're very glad you've come to meet us personally.

OXANA: Behave and I'll look after you. However, this attempt to escape this morning.

ANASTASIA: My sister was running. She fell.

OXANA: [*sarcastically in an aristocratic voice*] How she fell. My dear, how she almost flew out of the window!
TATIANA: Now I remember. I knew I recognised your face. You were in the palace.

> Pause. The GUARD is now fanning far more slowly. The thought process is: What?!

OXANA: Who was I? I don't remember.
TATIANA: That chamber maid.

> The GUARD stops fanning OXANA.

OXANA: The daughter of the imperial family has sharp eyes! Like their secret police. The Okhrana!
TATIANA: Oxana!
MARIA: [*dawning on her*] The one who was always staring at us. The lovelorn one.
ANASTASIA: Were you really a chamber maid from the palace?
GUARD: Chamber maid?
OXANA: [*with a shrug*] Like a caged bird I found my freedom. I stripped myself of every memory. Always an order. Go here. Be there. Wipe their mouths. All around, eyes watching you.
IVAN: [*putting on a posh voice*] What was the most stuck-up thing you ever did as a capitalist lackey, comrade?
OXANA: [*annoyed at losing the upper hand*] My mother brushed my hair a hundred times a day until …

> She stops herself—a psychic wound we discover later.

It's cake with butter. You'll soon be fat as pigs, comrades …

> She offers the cake in a royal gesture to no particular guard. IVAN steps in, again the GUARD pushes him aside.

If we eat it all up we won't have to report it.

> The GUARD carefully pulls the cake apart crumb by crumb.

GUARD: There may be a key hidden in it.

> The GUARD, having mauled the cake, takes some crumbs and eats them. OXANA now doesn't want to eat it anymore.

OXANA: Where is Olga Nikolaevna?

ANASTASIA: She's sitting with Alexei. Our brother is still sick. He now learns the violin to amuse himself.
OXANA: He was spoilt. Kicked my shins black and blue.
IVAN: When did you change sides, comrade?
OXANA: [*displaying how ideologically strong she is, yet with emotional truth*] An officer flogged me for wearing a red ribbon in the street. I saw Lenin as he stood waving on the balcony. I fell in love with him. The wind blowing blossoms, the first rays of sunlight spilling into my heart, the snows melting. I wasn't lost anymore. Lenin spoke like a true father, so I could see how I might fit in. We were family! I longed to belong. I took up arms for him, joined the Bolsheviks.
IVAN: Comrade!
OXANA: [*with a smile*] They promoted me here to the Regional Ural Committee.
GUARD: What am I to report in the files about the cake?
OXANA: I hate files. My mother reported me to the secret police.
TATIANA: I knew I knew you from the palace.
OXANA: Those servile days! My mother died alone. I didn't bury her. [*A warning to the girl*s] So many more must die like her.
ANASTASIA: You would make a good actor. How cleverly you have transformed yourself. And your language best of all!
TATIANA: [*deflecting from* ANASTASIA'*s provocation*] We would wave to the maids, from the mauve boudoir, blowing them kisses and giving them names.
IVAN: What's a boodwah, comrade?
OXANA: A fancy bedroom where her mother could lie around and sulk when she couldn't do what she pleased. Now I want to lie down.
TATIANA: [*taking advantage of* OXANA'*s mellowing with eating cake*] Please help us. It's so hot and these rooms are unbearably stuffy, the smells from that one filthy toilet.
MARIA: The mosquitoes are eating us alive ...
OXANA: Stop whining, girl, [*smiling*] like a mosquito. Even if it is a shithole.
GUARD: Ekaterinburg has a healthy climate. It's good to live here.
IVAN: It makes you strong if you survive it. We grew up, sweating in the foundries.
TATIANA: I remember you so vividly.

OXANA: [*taking control, angry*] Do you remember at night how Rasputin tucked you all up in bed in your little white nightdresses? How the Empress greeted him. Kiss me! Kiss me!

She grabs MARIA'*s jaw.*

How did he kiss you goodnight?

IVAN: [*suddenly breaking ranks*] Commissar Avadeyev hasn't issued a memorandum about touching up prisoners.

OXANA: [*turning on him*] *I* am second-in-command to the Commissar. Don't forget it.

GUARD: [*to* IVAN] Yes. Shut up, shithead.

OXANA: Or I will have you beaten for disobedience.

BOTKIN: God rest Grigori Rasputin's soul. Unwise to speak ill of the dead. [*Attempting to stop the argument*] You don't get rid of them that way. They haunt you.

ANASTASIA: He was our friend. Buried in the palace gardens.

TATIANA: Mama had the palace guards dig his grave like he was a saint.

ANASTASIA: So, he would always be there to protect us.

TATIANA: [*imperious*] If you're not careful you could end up like him— [*snapping her fingers*] finished.

On the snap of her fingers, OXANA *turns back to face* TATIANA.

OXANA: We soldiers of the revolution dug him up again. Burnt his body on the spot, so all the ashes flew into the four winds and no-one could pray to him anymore.

ANASTASIA: I'm beginning to forget our friend's face.

OXANA: There, there.

BOTKIN: You revolutionaries have to find a non-violent way to pull everyone out of misery and into a bright future for us all. Everyone deserves that.

OXANA: There, there … The doctor will go without his luncheon if you only let him talk philosophy.

BOTKIN: Kindly leave me alone.

The GUARD *wheels* BOTKIN *away from the girls.*

GUARD: [*in a feeble voice to* BOTKIN, *mimicking* OXANA'*s tone*] There, there, there.

BOTKIN: You're very dull company, you know.

ACT ONE

OXANA: To hell with the good old days [*to* IVAN, *who backs her up*] and the ruling class.

IVAN: Vile privileges.

A violin is played offstage—the playing of a youngster.

TATIANA: [*to* OXANA] That's Alexei practising.

NICHOLAS *enters. The violin's still squeaking and scraping.*

MARIA, ANASTASIA *and* TATIANA: [*in unison*] Papa.

Pause.

OXANA: Oxana, Commander in Charge to Commissar Avadeyev.

She holds out her hand to shake his, not easy because he was once the Tsar. NICHOLAS *ignores the extended hand and smacks his own hand as if a mosquito has landed on it.*

Citizen Romanov … I know.

NICHOLAS: You've come to live in the house?

OXANA: In the room, downstairs.

The violin stops.

Belt? You might hang yourself.

NICHOLAS *doesn't give up the belt yet, even though he knows she wants it.*

NICHOLAS: I should be in Moscow for my trial. Why am I here?

OXANA: Citizen. I interrogate you.

NICHOLAS: Citizen. I am sure you will do it well.

OXANA: Here, you need to remember, you are no longer the Tsar.

Pause as she is momentarily unsure how to proceed.

ANASTASIA: Just look what a nice photograph frame Father gave Maria today for her birthday. He made it himself.

OXANA: [*looking at the frame*] What knife did you use? That is a very nice knife with the imperial crest.

NICHOLAS: Please be my guest.

Pause. Their eyes meet. He takes off the knife, which is hanging on his belt, and presents it to her. NICHOLAS *then removes the belt.* OXANA *admires it and puts it on.*

You need it more than me. Such a small thing.

NICHOLAS *waves his hand and walks away.*

TATIANA: How could you do that?

NICHOLAS: It doesn't matter.

ANASTASIA: Don't go away, Papa! He's got into a habit of always going away. Come here, Papa!

TATIANA *and* ANASTASIA *take his arms and lead him back.*

NICHOLAS: Please leave me alone. Stop fussing! Dignity, girls.

GUARD: The Emperor must sit on his throne!

The GUARD *makes fun of* NICHOLAS *and makes him sit on one of the packing cases like it is a throne.* OXANA *becomes bolder.*

OXANA: The Citizen is shy.

She pulls a face, sending up NICHOLAS.

It's just a game!

GUARD: [*mimicking* OXANA *to* IVAN] Oxana was 'the lovelorn one' [*with much hilarity*] when she was in the palace.

OXANA: Not like him. The lovelorn husband. [*Taking the upper hand from the* GUARD] So in the latrine … [*to the naïve* IVAN] for you [*pretending to scrawl graffiti*] a picture of how Rasputin got his …

She laughs so much she can't get the word out.

GUARD: [*laughing*] As he and the Empress [*horseplay mimicry*] … wiped her clean with his beard.

BOTKIN: Nature only brought us into the world so we should love!

IVAN: I am in love!

The violin commences again offstage.

OXANA: What is that hideous screeching? Take it off that awful boy. He's doing it on purpose. I can't stand it.

She waves the GUARD *away, who exits.*

BOTKIN: How are you, sire?

NICHOLAS: [*wiping his face*] I couldn't sleep all night and my teeth ache.

OXANA: [*re the world and the violin*] It's giving me a splitting headache!

NICHOLAS: I felt it must be day when the sun crawled through a crack in the wall.

OXANA: We'll find something for you to do.

NICHOLAS: This summer, while I wait to go to Moscow for the trial, I want to translate a book [*taking* BOTKIN's *medical book, starting to glance at it*] from the English.

OXANA: English!

NICHOLAS: Yes, it is my wife's favourite language. I prefer Russian. My grandfather couldn't speak Russian.

TATIANA: [*glaring at* OXANA] Knowledge of many languages is pointless in this 'shithole'.

BOTKIN: [*wincing*] Tatiana!

MARIA: A sort of useless extra, like a sixth finger.

IVAN: [*crossing towards* MARIA] I wish I knew as much as you. This town could do with entertainment.

OXANA: What is that useless guard doing?

More screeching violin.

I can't hear myself think.

An abrupt stop to the violin as if it's been snatched from the player.

NICHOLAS *shares cake quietly and secretively from the plate* OXANA *left on the packing box with the girls.*

ANASTASIA: Chekhov came here once. He pulled the shutters down in his hotel, because he said Ekaterinburg was so ugly. That's all he ever said about this place and he was a famous playwright.

OXANA: She's like a parrot. Tchekov, Tchekov, Tchekov!

ANASTASIA: He didn't like it here at all.

IVAN: But now you have come here. It can't be such a bad place.

OXANA: Who cares?

NICHOLAS: I just lay awake last night thinking one thing after another.

IVAN: No need to worry. Because of Comrade Lenin life is going to be wonderful.

MARIA: Not ours.

Now in a half-kneel, IVAN *sits beside her.*

IVAN: Something very special about you.

TATIANA: [*sarcastic*] Next this hero will say, 'Your eyes are as big as saucers'.

IVAN: You don't really know who we are. Living in palaces looking down.

OXANA: [*to* IVAN] What's got into you? Is there some vodka somewhere?

IVAN: In the cellar. [*Looking at* MARIA] Because of the revolution we can all start again. There'll be food and love and happiness. Maybe ... [*still looking at* MARIA] or at least love.
MARIA: Is there cake for us?
OXANA: [*crossing to* MARIA] No food for you. In the corner. Turn your back!
MARIA: I'm not hungry anyway.
OXANA: [*to* IVAN] You watch her. She's not to move. What are the orders?
IVAN: Not to move.

>*The* GUARD *re-enters.*

OXANA: Bring us the best vodka! Now.

>*This is directed to* NICHOLAS, *who she wants to bring the vodka.*

NICHOLAS: In exchange for cigarettes?
OXANA: Yes. I will let the Revolutionary Committee know how comfortable you are here.

>OXANA *exits followed by* NICHOLAS, *who surreptitiously hands* MARIA *some of the cake on the plate as he passes by her.*

BOTKIN: Could there be a pie for lunch? Four and twenty blackbirds even better! Splendid! If only I could eat.
TATIANA: [*wheeling him out*] You must take the opiates if you need medicine. Don't keep it all for Mother and Father.

>TATIANA *and* ANASTASIA *wheel* BOTKIN *across the room, followed by the* GUARD.

BOTKIN: My kidneys are alright today.
TATIANA: You're to take it, all the same.
BOTKIN: It's not so bad.
GUARD: There, there, there.
BOTKIN: That's enough.
GUARD: There, there, there.

>*All exit, leaving* IVAN *and* MARIA. IVAN *upstage,* MARIA *downstage, on the diagonal, her back still turned.*

IVAN: I am in charge now. You are 'free' to be here with me.
MARIA [*quietly*] Why did you say you were in love?
IVAN: I wanted that repulsive woman ... to pull her claws in.

ACT ONE 15

MARIA: [*quietly*] Tatiana's out of sorts today too. She could have married when she was eighteen. Kings and Grand Dukes [*suddenly realising this is not what you say to a Bolshevik*] fell in love with her.

IVAN: A shoemaker or a butcher will have her now. Or maybe not. [*To himself*] She's so stuck-up.

MARIA: I once fell in love with an officer, but I only ever sent him a shirt I embroidered and then he disappeared in the war.

IVAN: If a girl embroidered me a shirt, I'd keep it forever.

He leans his rifle against the wall and crosses closer to her.

MARIA: [*half turning to him*] I don't know why I told you that.

She turns back.

IVAN: Did he want to marry you?

MARIA: I don't know.

IVAN: [*coming closer*] There's to be no more marriage. It's a bourgeois institution. Did you know? There's only love. Did he love you?

MARIA: I can't remember.

She fully turns, looking into his eyes. Not the coquette. Just looking.

IVAN: [*stepping in*] If he had any sense he would have.

Pause.

MARIA: Today [*to herself, but showing him her hand*] has been horrible.

IVAN: Today's been wonderful to me!

MARIA: [*smiling*] Not me.

IVAN: Everyone will have [*tying the bandage of ribbon on her hand*] whatever they need.

MARIA: I only care about love.

IVAN: Me too.

> MARIA *breaks away and sits on the packing case,* IVAN *stands behind her.*

MARIA: My parents made us behave as if only we mattered, our family and our beloved country … I'm crying. I don't even know how to live like you. My mother despises people like you …

IVAN: But she's German.

> IVAN *becomes flustered as* ALEXANDRA *enters. He crosses back and seizes his rifle.* ALEXANDRA*'s back is ramrod straight, yet her manner confused.*

ALEXANDRA: It takes time to prepare … I nearly didn't put in an appearance, my hands are shaking, I think my hair's satisfactory … I can't bear to have these guards watch us eat. I'd rather go back to my room!
MARIA: Mama, how are you feeling?
ALEXANDRA: You know I'm sick, my darling. *Bon anniversaire, ma chérie.* How inconceivably awful these people are. [*Indicating* IVAN] I mean look at him.

> MARIA *makes a half-hearted nod of agreement.* ANASTASIA *enters.*

ANASTASIA: [*in an undertone*] They took Papa's belt. Please don't say anything, Mama, don't!

> ALEXANDRA *clearly enunciates to* IVAN, *as if he is half-witted.*

ALEXANDRA: Is/ there/ food/ for/ luncheon?
ANASTASIA: There was cake. But they've eaten most of it.
ALEXANDRA: We must at least give thanks to God for food.

> *The sound of the violin scraping commences.* MARIA *and* ANASTASIA *exchange a look; however,* ALEXANDRA *sits and listens with a smile.* ANASTASIA *listens too, as she sits next to her mother.*

IVAN: [*to* MARIA, *anxious to escape* ALEXANDRA'*s eagle eye*] I can show you where there is some old black bread.
ALEXANDRA: Why should my darling girl have to go with that … that lout?

> IVAN *and* MARIA *exit as* OXANA *and* NICHOLAS *return. He holds the vodka.* ALEXANDRA, *still sitting, takes* NICHOLAS'*s hand. He stands in silence by her.* OXANA *grandly sits.*

OXANA: A thread binds us together. We must not forget that. But then a string makes us all puppets. Now, I am the puppet master, I can feel the strings.
ALEXANDRA: He's an ill-mannered oaf. Sweet Maria bravely went with him to find us bread.
OXANA: How the girls played with their ribbons. In the sunlight, chasing their butterflies. Show me!

> *The violin stops.*

ANASTASIA: If only we could fly to another world.

ACT ONE

OXANA: Silence! Play, girl!

> ANASTASIA *stands as if to 'play'.* ALEXANDRA *firmly takes her hand and pulls her back down to sit next to her on the packing case.*

> *The* GUARD *enters.* OXANA *hands one cigarette to the* GUARD, *who hands it to* NICHOLAS *and takes the vodka off him.* OXANA *and the* GUARD *toast each other with a shot of vodka.*

GUARD: To our visitor. We've hunted him down.
ALEXANDRA: So very unclean. We need a priest to bless the house.
OXANA: No monks in this house.
ALEXANDRA: *Mon dieu! Quelle horreur! Une femme en charge!*

> TATIANA *enters, wheeling* BOTKIN. *The dialogue starts to overlap.*

OXANA: No foreign languages. That's the new rule, 'madam'.
NICHOLAS: What rule?
OXANA: Only Lenin may speak in foreign language.
BOTKIN: What happens when you take over the world?

> *He exchanges a look with* NICHOLAS.

OXANA: Russian will be spoken *everywhere*.
NICHOLAS: Yes, I see your point. It will bring us all together.
ANASTASIA: I'm really hungry. My stomach's rumbling.
ALEXANDRA: [*to* ANASTASIA] Poor darling, you are looking *very pale*.
GUARD: Vampires!
ALEXANDRA: [*not listening, smiling at* ANASTASIA] *Je t'aime.*
OXANA: *No* foreign language.
GUARD: To comrades!
NICHOLAS: Is there anything nice to eat?
TATIANA: [*to* OXANA] If only we were on a train out of here. Steaming across the plains. Surely no-one will stop us. It's all misunderstanding, propaganda.
NICHOLAS: It's not easy to rule.
TATIANA: We need to get to Moscow for the trial.
ANASTASIA: [*loudly overriding the conversation*] We could perform Chekhov's *The Bear.*
GUARD: There's a bear downstairs. Stuffed. Waiting …
ANASTASIA: It's such a funny play.

OXANA: What about some revolutionary songs instead?
ALEXANDRA: I can't stand 'singalongs'.
OXANA: Was she always so dull? Or is it the drugs?
NICHOLAS: Please don't. Aren't you tired of it?
ALEXANDRA: The day you die you'll burn in hell.
OXANA: You poor deluded creature! Go and take more of that opium …

> OLGA *enters like a somnambulist. She holds a piece of old rye bread. It is like a dream vision. She drifts to the front, humming as she holds the bread. All is bathed in a different light. The scene becomes surreal.*

OLGA: Our friend Rasputin walks with me. In my waking dreams. Smell them! He says to me. Roast pig and potato. Berries of the forest. Tastes like raspberries, the pinkness of her cheeks. This crust of fine white bread is made from the millions who died to build Saint Petersburg. Feast on!

> MARIA *and* IVAN *enter. He follows her. She has a small basket of bread.* MARIA *offers bread to each.* ALEXANDRA *refuses the offering.* OLGA *drifts to the guards' exit. The* GUARD *waves her away.* OLGA *crosses to the front.* ALEXANDRA *follows and puts her arms around* OLGA. OLGA *crosses back upstage.*

ALEXANDRA: They're humiliating us. I can't bear it.

> *She sits on the packing case at the front of the stage, followed by* NICHOLAS.
>
> *The light dims to sunset.*

NICHOLAS: My dear, good sweet wife. They won't hurt us
ALEXANDRA: Those women are drunks. Holes in his clothes, the grime under his fingernails? Dripping sweat as he leaned on Maria's shoulder. It makes me sick. I need to lie down. I need my medicine. I suffered in the war too. Endless nights in the hospitals with the dying. The wounded men helpless. I did my best to soothe. [*Self-irony: I did all that, but now?!*] And now I need to wash myself. I feel so dirty. Is my hair untidy? [*Letting her hair fall*] Do you remember the fragrances, the rose, and the jasmine that used to cling to my hair? You loved my hair, bury your face in it. Run your fingers through it … [*Whispering*] Do you still love me, Nicky?

ACT ONE

NICHOLAS: Come here, they can't see us here inside or out.

ALEXANDRA: How can you still love me?

NICHOLAS: My darling, don't be so anxious! Believe me, believe me, my soul is full of love. They don't see us! But for the children and me, you must remain strong. My dear, my pure darling, my wife! I love you, love you ... as never before.

They kiss and embrace.

It will be alright.

OLGA *starts humming. The humming then starts to move from one to another, until all are humming*—BOTKIN, ANASTASIA, TATIANA, NICHOLAS. *It becomes like an evening at the dacha, each in their own world, remembering. Even* OXANA *shuts her eyes, remembering. The* GUARD *just stares ahead.*

Only IVAN *and* MARIA *look at each other and hum.*

NICHOLAS *exits.* ALEXANDRA *clips her hair up and exits upstage.* OLGA *exits to the kitchen. The sound of crashing pots and pans breaks the humming abruptly.*

Back to reality as the dream vision ends.

OXANA: [*standing, angrily to the girls, as if caught out*] What are you looking at? [*To* IVAN] Give that one a bucket of water from the kitchen. Let her scrub ... [*Waving in the direction of* MARIA] This one can stand in silence next to the toilet.

IVAN: That stinks.

TATIANA: It's bad enough we have to keep the toilet door open. Why do you make us do that?

BOTKIN: I really don't see why *they* should be made to scrub.

OXANA: [*to the* GUARD] Get rid of him!

The GUARD *wheels* BOTKIN *out.*

[*To* TATIANA] Not you. Sharp eyes. You come with me.

A lighting change.

ANASTASIA *is seated at the back.* IVAN *goes to get a bucket. The* GUARD *exits with* MARIA *and* BOTKIN. *The* GUARD *re-enters and moves back across the stage,* TATIANA *follows* OXANA *to the guards' exit.*

SCENE TWO

OLGA *enters.* KHARITONOV *enters with a fork/whisk in the saucepan, which sounds like a musical accompaniment as he hits the whisk against the saucepan. He is in his chef's whites.*

KHARITONOV: [*as if it's very sticky, and he feels lethargic*] I'm ... so hot.

OLGA: [*her memory triggered by* KHARITONOV*'s 'hot'*] It was hot when Papa and I sat in the opera box ... [*Then the recollection*] The Prime Minister stood up in the stalls. There was a gunshot. His hand all covered in blood, all over ... He collapsed and they dragged him from the theatre. I couldn't stop crying.

> KHARITONOV *exits, returning with a cup of water which he offers to* OLGA.

KHARITONOV: You must rest.

OLGA: I remember the opera music, softly melancholic, as the shot was fired. No-one could save him.

KHARITONOV: You must drink the water.

> *He holds the cup for* OLGA *to drink.*

Sip it slowly.

> IVAN *enters with a bucket which he places in front of* ANASTASIA.

ANASTASIA: I know we've been told we have to scrub. But I don't know how.

IVAN: [*laughing: That's impossible!*] Get on with it.

KHARITONOV: Why should she have to do such a menial task? She's not a maid.

IVAN: Show her how.

KHARITONOV: What! This is preposterous!

> KHARITONOV *exits and returns with a saucepan of noodles and a fork.*

IVAN: [*to* OLGA] Eh! You! Get up. No sitting around. Those days have gone.

OLGA: I will complain.

IVAN: Who to?

ACT ONE

KHARITONOV: [*ignoring* IVAN, *but with a smile to* ANASTASIA] Grand Duchess, let me offer you the last of the Empress's vermicelli noodles. They will give you strength.

He feeds her noodles from the saucepan with the fork.

You shouldn't work on an empty stomach.

ANASTASIA: There was a cake from outside. But they ate it!

KHARITONOV: Let me guess. Was it a simple Napoleonic gâteau with cream layers and a dollop of ice-cream?

ANASTASIA: It was strange. Flat like a brick.

IVAN: [*to* KHARITONOV *and* ANASTASIA, *loudly*] Stop!

He can't believe they are having this conversation as if he isn't there.

No eating! On your knees.

Pause. The following dialogue is very fast.

KHARITONOV: I will show her, sir.

IVAN: I'm not sir.

KHARITONOV: Whoever you are. How do you want to be addressed then?

IVAN: Comrade.

KHARITONOV: Comrade.

IVAN: That's right.

KHARITONOV: Comrade, I prefer to scrub the floor myself.

IVAN: [*realising he has made a mistake*] No. Citizen!

KHARITONOV: What?

IVAN: What about her?

KHARITONOV: Because I am showing the Grand Duchess—

IVAN: The citizen.

KHARITONOV: Alright then. The Citizen Grand Comrade how to—

IVAN: [*to* OLGA *as she hums again*] What are you doing?

OLGA: I am a prisoner.

IVAN: Right. Not a comrade. It's citizen. Get a brush for her too. Show her.

KHARITONOV: Apologies, Citizen Comrade Grand Duchesses.

IVAN: [*to* OLGA, *getting her attention*] Eh, you! Scrub.

OLGA: What?

ANASTASIA: Olga could sing. It'll help.

IVAN: How?
ANASTASIA: Isn't that what peasants do? Sing as they work?
IVAN: Get on with it!

> KHARITONOV *starts to scrub.* OLGA *sings, gradually getting faster and faster.*

KHARITONOV: Like this. You dip the brush in the water.
ANASTASIA: [*with interest*] It's filthy black.
KHARITONOV: And go back and forth over the lumps of grease.

> *She does this.*

Some of them are so old they stick to the floor.
ANASTASIA: [*enthusiastically, as an actress studying a new part*] I'll have to dig at them with my nails. This place is infested with cockroaches.
KHARITONOV: You're disturbing them.

> *He swipes at two with his tea towel—thwack, thwack on the floor.*

Grand Duchess, be careful of yourself in the heat.
IVAN: Now the Commissar will be pleased. Everyone working and building up a sweat.
ANASTASIA: It smells horrible.
KHARITONOV: This is heartless.
ANASTASIA: My name …

> *She stops* OLGA'*s singing with her hand, and announces:*

… is now Natalya!

> KHARITONOV *looks bewildered.*

KHARITONOV: Who?
ANASTASIA: [*with a heavy accent*] But you can call me Natasha! She is unmarried, longs to find a husband, [*looking at* IVAN *and* KHARITONOV] wears a yellow dress with black spots. Now with rheumatism she scrubs! Music!

> *She jumps on the packing case helped by* IVAN *and* KHARITONOV *on either side of her. She takes the tea towel off* KHARITONOV'*s shoulder and puts it on her head like a kerchief.*
>
> *The sound of a silent movie piano. Flickering lights.* OLGA *picks up the saucepan of noodles and starts to eat them as she watches the others. We are now in* ANASTASIA'*s silent movie. It will be*

played in silent movie style. Projected onto the walls are the following subtitles in sequence to the action, in both English and Cyrillic:
   'OH! COCKROACHES!'
ANASTASIA, *as the film heroine, strikes a pose of horror,* IVAN *and* KHARITONOV *pose as cockroaches.*
   'DEATH!'
The heroine takes off her kerchief and strangles IVAN *the cockroach.* KHARITONOV *the cockroach looks on in horror.*
   'MERCY!'
IVAN *the cockroach is on his back curled up on the floor.* KHARITONOV *the cockroach begs on his knees, hands in prayer, for mercy.*
   'VICTORY!'
The piano music cuts out. The projected titles finish. KHARITONOV *and* IVAN *get to their feet.*

But ANASTASIA *still holds the pose of victory.*

The two men are now engaging in friendly conversation.

KHARITONOV: I am so sorry, Grand—
IVAN: What are you apologising for?
KHARITONOV: This breaks my heart.
IVAN: Citizen, this is for your own good.
KHARITONOV: Yes, sir.
IVAN: Don't call me sir.
KHARITONOV: No, sir.
IVAN: I am Ivan [*putting his hand out*] Sokhorov.
KHARITONOV: [*shaking it, introducing himself*] Kharitonov. Sir … Sokhorov.

   He puts his arm around IVAN*'s shoulders and offers* IVAN *the saucepan of noodles.*

Please eat up the last of the Empress's vermicelli noodles before they congeal.

   A change of speed, as order is re-established.

IVAN: I've never eaten this.
KHARITONOV: Dear boy, partake, eat your fill, if all is to be shared, be our guest.

IVAN: I'll take some home to mother.
KHARITONOV: They need to be eaten hot.

> MARIA *enters, laughing as she looks at* ANASTASIA *in her monumental pose.*

MARIA: How funny *you* look!

> ANASTASIA *looks annoyed and steps down from the packing case.*

ANASTASIA: You don't understand art anyway!

> ANASTASIA *seizes* KHARITONOV*'s hand and marches off.*

MARIA: [*to* IVAN] How funny *you* look! With noodles hanging from your mouth.
IVAN: What's wrong with that?
MARIA: You wrap them around the fork like this.
IVAN: Mmm.
MARIA: Why do you hate us?
IVAN: I don't hate you. How could I hate you? I like you.

> *He gives her some of the noodles on his fork.*

MARIA: There must be girls outside you like better?
IVAN: No. Not one.

> *The* GUARD *enters, crossing the stage, surprised to see* IVAN *and* MARIA.

GUARD: [*to* IVAN, *threatening*] What are you doing? This will have to be reported.

> *The* GUARD *promptly exits and* IVAN *follows.* MARIA *runs to the rooms offstage.*

END OF ACT ONE

ACT TWO

SCENE ONE

Three weeks later. It is dark. In the far distance there is the sound of cannons and gunfire. Lights flicker.

OXANA *and* TATIANA *are at the front of the stage.* OXANA, *with vodka, pours a shot for each of them.* TATIANA *throws her drink back and grimaces.*

TATIANA: Do you know Rasputin prophesied our circumstances would change and they have.

OXANA: I can hear the train in the distance. Moving the army.

TATIANA: When we are freed we will do what we like again.

OXANA: Soon we will be trapped by the Whites. Your people.

TATIANA: As for the other people! I don't speak of any particular guard, but they are so often coarse, and rude. Why do women want to join up?

OXANA: They need us. In your whole life, I bet you never screamed or shouted once.

Pause. She looks into TATIANA*'s eyes. She goes to pour her another drink, but* TATIANA *places her hand across the glass.*

TATIANA: Rasputin never screamed. It was wealthy men who poisoned him with cakes, shot him and he ran away. Clubbed him over the head. Wrapped his body in chains and threw him in the icy river and held his head under the water. Only then did he drown with his mouth open.

OXANA: A black magician. Did he give you magic?

TATIANA: He gave us lockets.

She leans forward and shows the locket around her neck. OXANA *breathes in her warmth.*

To protect us. Listen to the silence, he said, that is best.

Guns sound.

OXANA: Ah!

> *Pause as she considers this.*

It's dark here, but when you smile the world lights up!

TATIANA: [*quickly moving across centre stage and turning her back on* OXANA] A trick of the light.

> *Following* TATIANA, OXANA *grabs her arms, turning her around to face her.*

OXANA: Tell me about who you know among the Whites that are coming. I want to help you. If I help you, your friends will help me.

TATIANA: If you let us live, our friends will support you.

OXANA: I have kept you here safe and made sure no harm came to you.

TATIANA: We will be free.

OXANA: But my guards and I would need a reward. What about gold, furs, diamonds?

> OXANA *kisses her forehead.*

TATIANA: [*escaping upstage through the upstage exit*] Somebody's coming.

> OXANA *exits through the guards' exit as* IVAN *enters.* MARIA *steps in through the upstage left entrance.*

MARIA: Where are you going?

> *Their eyes meet.*

IVAN: Where are you going?

MARIA: To sit with Mama. She is unwell.

IVAN: Stay!

MARIA: What for?

> *They move centre stage.*

IVAN: When have you been the most scared?

MARIA: You?

IVAN: I stole this for you! A little gold knife from the guard's room today. [*Conspiratorially*] I've never seen one like this before … look at it … three blades, scissors …

> *Pause.*

What's that?

ACT TWO

MARIA: Tweezers.
IVAN: Tweezers.
MARIA: It's a nail cleaner.
IVAN: How does it work?
MARIA: [*laughing*] I'll show you.

> MARIA *takes* IVAN's *hand and carefully cleans his nails under the following dialogue.*

IVAN: When have you been scared?
MARIA: When you all attacked the palace at night. I walked out in the snow in my nightdress. The snowflakes sticking to my eyelashes [*coquettish*] blinding me. Our soldiers knelt there, but they were ready to run. I begged them in the blizzard. Please protect us, don't abandon my family. [*Throwing this away, lightly*] I nearly died of pneumonia out there.
IVAN: That is heroic.
MARIA: I felt like I was burning up inside.
IVAN: They say we shouldn't think about you, but it's hard. We talk about you and I think about you off duty. All the guards here like you and think about you.
MARIA: I would like to be free to walk hand in hand with my true love. Whenever I want.
IVAN: [*thinking, then crossing downstage and around her*] What if he was sent alone on horseback to some wasteland?
MARIA: I'd follow him.
IVAN: What if it's freezing? You'd have to ride. To keep warm.
MARIA: Ride.

> *Together they ride on the spot like a game, laughing.*

IVAN: You are not to let anyone know about this.
MARIA: I won't breathe a word.
IVAN: Your sisters, mother, father.

> *They ride side by side on the spot, unified in this game.*

MARIA: I won't.
IVAN: In your rags, with bracelets and trinkets like any poor girl, you look good to me.
MARIA: Do I?

IVAN: You could not have looked better even if you were covered in gold and diamonds.
MARIA: And you to me, even though you are not dressed like a proper soldier.
IVAN: They will kill us if they know.
MARIA: I know.
IVAN: I'm not a traitor.
MARIA: [*stopping riding*] I am.
IVAN: [*getting off his horse*] What class enemy?
MARIA: No. Loving someone more than Papa.
IVAN: What do you mean?
MARIA: It's like fire in my heart.
IVAN: I'd cut off anyone's fingers who hurt you. How long your eyelashes are!
MARIA: They flutter like a butterfly.

    She brushes his cheek with her lashes.

IVAN: Like my heart.
MARIA: What do lovers do now?
IVAN: They lie down in the grass.
MARIA: Rest their heads on each other's shoulders.
IVAN: But they don't sleep.

    MARIA *and* IVAN *kiss.* OXANA *enters, noticing them. They spring apart.*

OXANA: I won't say a thing.

    She walks on.

Until the next time.

    Lighting change.

SCENE TWO

IVAN *with a rifle. The bucket from the scrubbing scene is still behind the packing case.*

Phantasmagoric. Night-time. Darkness, except for a spotlight which captures each of the characters in pairs or separately.

Spotlight one:

ACT TWO

ALEXANDRA: Such a still, hot night!
ANASTASIA: I shouldn't mind the weather if I were performing at the Moscow Art Theatre.
ALEXANDRA: Anna ... you need to broaden your interests. Is my hair alright? They don't make officers like they once did. I chose twenty-five Imperial Guards for the imperial ball and how we danced. I dressed as a peasant in minks and ermines and diamonds as big as eggs. It was the talk of Saint Petersburg.

Spotlight two:

IVAN: [*quietly to* MARIA] If anything happens.
MARIA: What if you are arrested? I feel this little knife has sliced my heart.
IVAN: It didn't happen.
MARIA: If we go to Moscow for the trial you'll still be here, thousands of miles away. There will be no love for us. Maybe love is only a dream.
IVAN: You'll forget me. That I was here with you.

Spotlight three:

TATIANA: Why are you so silent?
OXANA: I don't know. Something's not right. My gut feels queasy. I need vodka.

She toasts.

Half my life for a shot of vodka.

Spotlight four:

BOTKIN: Anastasia!
ANASTASIA: What is it?
BOTKIN: As a doctor, it's my duty to do what others find abhorrent. We will resurrect Chekhov's *The Bear* and I will learn the lines.
ANASTASIA: Let me count the ways I love you.
BOTKIN: You know, if the Revolution succeeds people will go insane, raving on and on more and more like the lunatics who govern them, maybe one day they'll discover a sixth sense and develop it, but life will remain the same. Everyone wants someone to kick around.

Spotlight five:

TATIANA: All people are just as afraid of death, and unwilling to meet it, as we are.

OXANA: We decide who lives and dies. We of the Committee are in charge. No-one else. Not Moscow. Not Lenin, not Trotsky.

Spotlight six:

ALEXANDRA: Do you remember when Olga was sixteen, she had her first ball at our beautiful palace overhanging the cliffs on the Black Sea? How you all loved to lie on its marble floors listening to the waves. The scent of roses floating in the night air under the stars. Memories so precious they can't be stolen by them. Grandpapa was sunning himself in the warmth eating ice cream though it was forbidden for his health. Then he died suddenly. After there was a huge storm. Your papa said I don't want to be Emperor and he cried. Now he's Emperor no more. He's got his wish.

Spotlight seven:

BOTKIN: Whatever happens to us, life will follow its own laws. Migrant birds, cranes fly and fly, and whatever thoughts enter their heads, they will still fly and not know why. They fly and will continue to fly, whatever revolutionaries come to life among them; the cranes may even turn red if they like, only they will go on flying ...

Spotlight eight:

TATIANA: Isn't there some meaning?

OXANA: [*more courteously*] The only meaning is the Revolution. And love.

TATIANA: To live and not to know where the wind goes, why there are stars in the sky, why babies are born.

OXANA: Would you like a child? I could see that belly round and soft. I could arrange it as a way out of here.

The entrance of the GUARD *brings all back to reality.*

The lights change.

GUARD: [*to* OXANA] There's a message for you. Just came.

He offers her a note.

OXANA: For me?

She takes the note.

From the Committee.

She reads, before standing up, agitated.

ACT TWO

To hell with this.

IVAN: What is it?

OXANA: [*ignoring him, to the* GUARD] I'm dead. Go downstairs, to the street. I'll follow shortly.

The GUARD *exits, as* OXANA *has a drink.*

ANASTASIA: Let's rehearse the play now.

OXANA: There will be no more plays.

ANASTASIA: Oh, that is so unfair. Why?

OXANA: The matter is decided.

ANASTASIA: I thought you were in charge.

OXANA: We all need to watch our backs.

ANASTASIA: Now you want to take our souls prisoner too.

OXANA: I don't want to hear any more.

ANASTASIA: You don't understand art anyway. I hate her.

ALEXANDRA: [*to* OXANA] It would be much better if instead of standing outside and gawking at our fortified house—'Is the Emperor in there, is he? Can we have a photograph of the Tsarina?'—that the townspeople stormed this place. They appear to be utterly moronic in this part of the world. Tati, I need my medicine and my hair needs doing.

ALEXANDRA *exits, followed by* TATIANA.

OXANA: [*to* IVAN, *getting a shot of vodka*] Why are you and her always together?

IVAN: Let's make peace.

OXANA: Why?

IVAN: There's been enough killing.

OXANA: I haven't quarrelled with you.

IVAN: There's been enough killing without one comrade turning against the other.

OXANA *takes his rifle off him. She strokes it.*

OXANA: I put a bullet through my mother's head. I wiped out the informer.

Pause, as the shock of this information is digested. A dead silence hangs as NICHOLAS *enters quietly with a book. He sits next to* ANASTASIA *and does not acknowledge* OXANA, *who sits on the packing case stage right.*

Ah! Citizen Romanov!

IVAN: All power to Trotsky and the trial in Moscow!
BOTKIN: It's a family feud. Lenin hates the Tsar because he hanged Lenin's brother.
OXANA: It's a holy war. Oppressed against the oppressor.
IVAN: Yes!
OXANA: What's mine is mine?

> IVAN *boldly crosses to* OXANA *and sits next to her.*

IVAN: Whatever happens, happens. Let's drink.

> OXANA *pours him a drink.*

OXANA: [*toasting*] Workers of the world unite!
IVAN: [*toasting*] You have nothing to lose but your chains.
OXANA: If you survive. I wouldn't want to see you digging up roots and grasses.

> *She hands* IVAN *his rifle back.*

BOTKIN: [*to* NICHOLAS] If only Kharitonov could make a real Caucasian onion soup, your health would improve, and, for a roast, some chehartma.
OXANA: [*standing*] Chehartma isn't meat at all, it's onion.
BOTKIN: It isn't onion, [*wheeling across to* OXANA] it's roast mutton.
OXANA: No, it's onion.
BOTKIN: Mutton!
OXANA: Grandpa—onion.
BOTKIN. What's the use of arguing?!
OXANA: You … you sick old man, I'll make you walk to the Caucasus.
BOTKIN: You're not from the Caucasus, and never ate any chehartma.
OXANA: [*pushing the wheelchair backwards, her face close to* BOTKIN*'s*] I never ate it, because I hate it. It smells like garlic. Only traitors eat that muck and will die with it stuck in their mouths.

> *She gives him a push offstage.*

NICHOLAS: [*imploring*] Please, please! I ask you!
OXANA: [*back to her seat*] What?
NICHOLAS: When/ is/ the play?
ANASTASIA: She has forbidden it.

> NICHOLAS *takes this information in. His jaw sets.* BOTKIN *wheels back on.*

ACT TWO

OXANA: Citizen Romanov! Sing us a song instead.

> *In her attempt to humiliate him,* NICHOLAS *turns the situation with his wit.* ANASTASIA *cottons on to what he is doing.* NICHOLAS *hums 'brpp brpp' in a military way. He stands and starts to march, like a clockwork soldier.* ANASTASIA *joins in behind him, another clockwork soldier.*

BOTKIN: Hang it all, let's drink. Sire, let's drink to you. I'll go with you to Moscow, and for your trial we will find lawyers at the University of Moscow.

> ANASTASIA *joins in behind* NICHOLAS *in the marching, singing game, like follow the leader.*

OXANA: Which one? There are two universities in Moscow.

NICHOLAS: There's only one decent university in Moscow.

OXANA: Two, I tell you.

NICHOLAS: Two. Two. Two. So much the better … [*like a train*] too-toot!

> MARIA *joins in too, creating a conga line of the train. The movement becomes circular.* OXANA *is furious—her command is being subverted and challenged.*

OXANA: [*shouting*] The new one and the old one! The Bolsheviks and the new way! The former people and the old way! We will tear the pages out of your books!

IVAN: Trotsky wants books for the poor.

> IVAN *laughs and joins in the conga line, putting a hand on* MARIA*'s waist.* NICHOLAS *holds his hands out to stop. They pile up as he and the two girls fall laughing.*

> *As* NICHOLAS *gets up on all fours,* OXANA *takes her opportunity and jumps on his back. The others look on in shock.*

OXANA: How about a horse? The poor need a horse. I need a horse.

MARIA: Stop it!

OXANA: Go on, neigh.

NICHOLAS: It's only a bit of fun.

OXANA: Whinny.

NICHOLAS: [*to himself, on all fours*] Charades.

OXANA: Louder. Or I'll whip you!

NICHOLAS *whinnies and neighs.*

[*Kicking her heels hard into* NICHOLAS] Faster.

MARIA: [*screaming*] *Get off Papa!*

> NICHOLAS *bucks and throws* OXANA *off his back. He is still in game mode and puts his hand out to help her up.*

OXANA: Who do you think I am? A servant? To disrespect me? You are my property.

> OXANA *throws the bucket of dirty scrubbing water over* NICHOLAS. *She exits.*

ANASTASIA: Papa! You are soaking wet.

NICHOLAS: Don't breathe a word of this to your mother. Her nerves are shattered.

ANASTASIA: You fell over the bucket I left there. We'll say you tripped.

> ANASTASIA *helps* NICHOLAS *out the upstage exit.* BOTKIN *is still upstage left.*

IVAN: [*calling after* NICHOLAS] Say you were drunk!

> *The sound of a lone mosquito.*

MARIA: Let's enjoy ourselves as if nothing happened.

> MARIA *and* IVAN *look at each other, totally ignoring the presence of* BOTKIN. IVAN *props his gun against the guards' exit.*

IVAN: Show me how to dance.

MARIA: [*whispering*] You can hold me close.

> *Taking his hand,* MARIA *teaches* IVAN *to dance.*

One, two, three, one, two, three … [*As if remembering waltz music*] It's not so hard. Our first waltz.

> *Gradually the tentative dance becomes more ecstatic as if they have developed wings as they dance in circles, in a flight of imagination—bigger, bolder. Poetic space.* MARIA *as if hearing waltz music which floods the stage. As for* BOTKIN, *he has seen it all—war, revolution and now this.*

> ALEXANDRA *comes in and watches the dance in horror, unnoticed by the dancers.*

ACT TWO

ALEXANDRA: [*to the dancers*] What are you doing?! Stop that!

> IVAN *nervously jumps apart from* MARIA, *as* NICHOLAS *enters, followed by* ANASTASIA.

What is that awful smell of garlic?

> IVAN *crosses behind her quickly to retrieve his rifle.*

NICHOLAS: I dropped my cigarette, my clothes started to burn, and they dowsed me in water.

ALEXANDRA: What is the matter with you all?

> *She looks angrily at* MARIA. *Says something in* NICHOLAS'*s ear as she kisses his cheek.*

[*Whispering*] Tonight's the night.

> ALEXANDRA *sweeps out.*

ANASTASIA: What is it?

NICHOLAS: Time to go to bed. [*Yawning, in an exaggerated way, to get rid of* IVAN] Goodnight.

ANASTASIA: You only just got up.

IVAN: It's time I went on duty outside.

> *He goes to exit, but turns back to look at* MARIA. *She crosses to him. All watch, then turn their eyes away.* IVAN *kisses* MARIA'*s hand.*

But I'll come back. Wait for me.

> IVAN *bows to her and exits.*

NICHOLAS: You see girls ... tonight might be the night ... we may be rescued.

MARIA: Who will rescue us, what about Ivan? Can he come with us if he can be persuaded to changes sides?

ANASTASIA: [*caught up in the drama of that idea*] Oh yes!

NICHOLAS: Where are the cigarettes? I need a cigarette to think, [*to* MARIA] but don't put too much faith in it.

ANASTASIA: Let's talk to Ivan outside.

> ANASTASIA *exits, following* IVAN.

NICHOLAS: I don't think that's wise. Just let me calm down and have a smoke.

MARIA: He will help us, Papa.

NICHOLAS: You must be dressed and ready to go. No word of our plans to anyone, including that young man, not till the rescue takes place.
BOTKIN: What's the matter, sire?
NICHOLAS: I don't feel very well. What am I to do for my asthma? In these wet clothes, I feel [*as if it's hard to breathe*] ... as if I'm gasping for breath.
MARIA: I want to get married one day.
BOTKIN: I managed to get married but rarely saw my wife and children, because the Empress demanded I was never away.
NICHOLAS: One should marry because it's a joy.
BOTKIN: My wife had an affair, because I was never there. What else could I do but divorce her?
NICHOLAS: I need to be calm. My stomach is in knots.
BOTKIN: I will give you the medicine that is left.
NICHOLAS: I'm afraid my wife takes too much morphine, yet she wants to stop me.
BOTKIN: Ah!
NICHOLAS: Wifey is in pain. I don't want her to be an addict. What am I to do for my asthma?
BOTKIN: Don't ask me! I don't remember ... I don't know.
MARIA: What about *my* marriage?
NICHOLAS: Let's go through the kitchen. Tell Kharitonov he must stay dressed when he goes to bed.

> *He grabs* MARIA*'s hand, and they exit with* BOTKIN.
>
> *The stage is empty.* MARIA *runs back in, picks up the knife and follows* ANASTASIA*'s exit off. As she does,* OXANA *enters, stripped of Nicholas's belt. A black eye. Bloody mouth. Now in a different capacity. Broken.* MARIA *senses* OXANA *is in trouble.*

OXANA: [*with wet eyes, emotional*] There's nobody here. Where are they all?
MARIA: They've gone to bed.
OXANA: Strange.

> *A pause.* MARIA, *taught to serve those in distress, is kind.* OXANA *opens* MARIA*'s hand that holds the knife.*

[*Wanting contact*] Who stole this? This is my knife.
MARIA: No. It's Papa's.

ACT TWO

OXANA: And I tell you it is mine. Give it back. [*Almost weeping*] The Romanovs stole from the people of Russia. Nothing belongs to them anymore. It's mine.
MARIA: [*gently*] Much good may it do you.
OXANA: When I stood inside the palace, it was you I loved, that little girl on the staircase looking down at me.
MARIA: I have to go now.
OXANA: I wanted to steal you and take you home.
MARIA: Stop it!
OXANA: [*sad, kissing* MARIA*'s hands*] I don't want the men to take you …

> ALEXANDRA *enters. The roar of a truck outside the house.*

ALEXANDRA: What are you doing here with Maria? She's not for the likes of you.
OXANA: [*staring at* ALEXANDRA] I smoothed her hair. Dabbed her with perfume. While you obsessed about that boy.
ALEXANDRA: You disgust me.

> OXANA *crosses away to the packing case stage right.*

[*To* MARIA] You … you are no daughter of mine. I disown you. Even Rasputin loved you the best, called you his little pearl, his sweet pear. But you are rotten. All of us no longer in God's grace since he was murdered.
OXANA: You didn't give any of us what we needed.

> ALEXANDRA *is shocked, but then suddenly registers the sounds of the truck outside.*

ALEXANDRA: It's a miracle. The trucks have come. Our friend is here in spirit with us. We are to be rescued. Get ready! Quickly! Tatiana!

> ANASTASIA *enters.*

Get the pillows. Take whatever you can! Hurry!
ANASTASIA: It's the Reds. They took Ivan. It's the Reds.
ALEXANDRA: [*to* MARIA] This is you! This is your punishment!

> ALEXANDRA *sweeps out.*

ANASTASIA: They pushed him in the back of the truck. They grabbed his head. Blindfolded him. Beating him. They hit the back of his head with a rod. Blood seeped through his shirt. It was the Reds. They drove away. They've gone. They're not coming back.

MARIA, *catatonic with shock, sits on the packing case at the back.* ANASTASIA *exits.* KHARITONOV *enters, oblivious to all that has happened. He sits next to her.*

KHARITONOV: Where has the Empress gone? Would she like me to rustle up a hot toddy for her aches and pains? [*Complaining to* MARIA] The less one has to do the more tired one becomes. And there's only one egg left. The guards have stolen all the others.

OXANA: Where is Tatiana?

KHARITONOV: Gone to bed.

OXANA: Go, get her.

KHARITONOV: I feel so weary. I'm afraid to sleep. I have nightmares. Not a scrap of food to be seen.

KHARITONOV *exits.*

MARIA: Where has Ivan gone? Do you know about the truck?

OXANA: Don't ask questions.

MARIA: Was it you who arranged it?

OXANA: Look at me!

MARIA: Where will they take him?

OXANA: The front. To fight! The Whites are coming closer to rescue you.

MARIA: Why him?

OXANA: Why any of us? It's fate.

TATIANA *enters.*

TATIANA: What do you want?

OXANA: Someone complained to the secret police I was too interested in one of the girls here.

MARIA: What will the secret police do to Ivan?

OXANA: Without gold … What can you still give me?

MARIA: [*taking the locket from her neck*] It's of Rasputin. We are meant to keep the lockets so even in death we are bound together. But a guard stole Alexei's.

OXANA: [*biting it*] I like this. A pure gold necklace.

MARIA: Use this to help Ivan. Don't let them kill him.

TATIANA: Rasputin will protect you with his magic.

OXANA: Hah! The Whites didn't kill me. But the Reds might.

TATIANA: Why would the Reds kill you?

ACT TWO

OXANA: Because I gave *you* privileges. They said I should be shot. Hard labour for ten years.

> *She holds her hand out to shake* TATIANA*'s hand.* TATIANA, *rather than shaking hands, gives her her hand to hold.* OXANA *presses it against her heart.*

I'll always remember you sharp eyes. Pity you weren't the Empress.

> OXANA *exits.*

MARIA: I'll go and lie down. I will find Ivan. We will run away [*exiting*] and no-one will ever find us.

TATIANA: We have to get to Moscow!

> *Guns and heavy artillery are heard in the distance.*

END OF ACT TWO

ACT THREE

A few weeks later. The sound of alarm bells ringing.

On one side, OLGA *sits on the floor.* TATIANA *and* ANASTASIA *sit on dirty mattresses on the other side, winding ribbons with the odd ring concealed in them, making sashes.*

KHARITONOV *enters from the upstage left entrance.*

KHARITONOV: They are hammering down windows and putting in alarms.

> *He indicates a bell attached to his wrist.*

It's madness.

> MARIA *enters the kitchen area.*

MARIA: I feel ill. Do you have anything to settle my stomach?

KHARITONOV: [*patting his chef's jacket and trousers*] Not even a potato. I've heard whispers the White Army is a few miles from town. Those Reds will be kicked out. We will be saved. I'm so tired.

OLGA: You need more rest.

> KHARITONOV *sits on the floor next to* OLGA.

KHARITONOV: Olga, my dear Duchess, don't let the Bolsheviks send me away.

OLGA: [*distantly*] Why would they send you away?

KHARITONOV: My heart. Where will I go? Where? In this town? They will hang me …

MARIA: Quiet.

KHARITONOV: The guards shouted, 'Why do the dirty bourgeois need so many baths? But they'll only get clean when we hang them from the hooks.'

MARIA: They will hear you.

KHARITONOV: If I leave here, Yurovsky the Commissar says I will have to live in the country. The Bolsheviks wouldn't want any unnecessary people here or in Moscow.

MARIA: [*to* KHARITONOV] You're tired, poor thing!

ACT THREE

KHARITONOV: What is the world coming to?!
OLGA: He's not clever enough to hide.

> *Pause.* IVAN *stands with bare feet in the doorway where he once stood. No-one sees him, only* OLGA. *She hums the waltz tune to which* IVAN *and* MARIA *danced. She continues until* IVAN *goes.*

MARIA: What about Ivan?
OLGA: I can see him bleeding. His face kicked in. Our friend showed me. I wasn't dreaming.
MARIA: Is Ivan calling for me?
OLGA: He's dying.
MARIA: You're making it up.
OLGA: He didn't obey the rules.
KHARITONOV: You must obey the rules.
OLGA: He's a prisoner too. That's the truth.
MARIA: Stop it. It's just in your head.

> *All look at* YUROVSKY *as he enters in a long black leather coat. The* GUARD *follows and remains upstage. All stand except* OLGA *who remains sitting on the floor.*

KHARITONOV: It is hard for an old man to be made to sleep on the floor.
YUROVSKY: What about the workers who were made to sleep under their machines on the factory floor?
KHARITONOV: Their bones would ache like mine.
YUROVSKY: [*to* OLGA] Why do you spend your days with him?
OLGA: Because servants care for me. He cares about me.
MARIA: She thinks she sees things. She doesn't know anything.
YUROVSKY: What do you talk about together?

> *The* GUARD *begins to write the answer down, but* YUROVSKY *stops this with a hand gesture.*

KHARITONOV: The cake box with a large velvet bow, inside are macaroons and bonbons. A special treat I made when the four grand duchesses painted in the gardens. The Empress only ever wanted bread and butter for tea. Like the English.
YUROVSKY: [*ironically*] Life is hard. I understand.

> *He sits on the packing case behind* OLGA.

I was driven out of Russia because of my political views. But you see how my life has changed.

OLGA: You are on the winning side.
YUROVSKY: There is the White Army fighting to rescue you. You know nothing of that?
OLGA: No. I never want to leave Russia.
YUROVSKY: [*changing tone, rapidly*] Now we will disinfect the House of Special Purpose.

> *He slaps* KHARITONOV *hard on the back and follows him as he exits upstage into the family quarters offstage.*

GUARD: [*in a threatening gesture to* KHARITONOV] Move!

> *In the lighting change,* IVAN *is no longer seen.* OLGA *hums the last echo of the waltz.*

> MARIA *crosses and sits on the packing case upstage. Sitting on the mattresses,* TATIANA *and* ANASTASIA *continue to wrap the few pieces of jewellery, hidden in strips of cloth lying in a jumble.*

TATIANA: We can't hide these. This one's ripped—if they see a jewel, they'll be suspicious. Tie this one on me … We mustn't be frightened or there'll be nothing left by the time we are freed.
MARIA: What are you doing?
TATIANA: None of your business.

> *The sounds of alarm bells and hammering offstage.*

MARIA: How awful this noise is. I'm sick of it!
TATIANA: [*to* ANASTASIA] Let them have this icon, say it's all we have left.

> ANASTASIA *exits. The violin is heard playing offstage.*

MARIA: What about our bangles so tight around our wrist they will have to cut them off?

> TATIANA *ignores her.* ALEXANDRA *enters and takes centre stage. She circles the room.*

ALEXANDRA: They are saying more bars are to be placed across our bedroom window. It's a sign there are people who want to help us, rescue us. I suppose my hair is untidy. I'm growing old, how grey my hair is. [*To* MARIA *sharply, but with her back to her*] Why are you sitting down?
MARIA: I need to.

ACT THREE

ALEXANDRA: You shouldn't be sitting down at this hour.

    ANASTASIA *re-enters.*

ANASTASIA: We all have to be here together. Yurovsky wants to inspect each room personally.

ALEXANDRA: I don't want any of you talking to Maria. [*Turning to face* MARIA] Now get up!

MARIA: Leave me alone. I'm sick.

    TATIANA *stands, as does* ANASTASIA.

TATIANA: Don't talk to Mama like that.

ALEXANDRA: Your sisters don't want you in here.

MARIA: I'll sit with Olga then.

ALEXANDRA: Ignore her. Chin up, we will be rescued.

    She reaches out to touch OLGA *who shrinks away.*

MARIA: [*to* OLGA] Why can't you bear to be touched?

ALEXANDRA: [*interrupting, she picks up a shawl and places it around* OLGA] What if there's a cholera outbreak? Is that why Yurovsky wants the place disinfected? I'm afraid Baby may catch it. Oxana was so dirty and all her guards, if it's not cholera it'll be typhoid.

MARIA: No-one is going to rescue us.

ALEXANDRA: [*coldly*] Get up! Out of this room. I don't want to hear your nasty lies. God will save us. We need to keep our minds and hearts clean for when we enter Paradise.

TATIANA: Yurovsky wants to return the goods Oxana stole from each of us.

MARIA: She didn't steal from Olga.

ANASTASIA: It can't be returned anyhow. It's gone forever in that railway carriage.

MARIA: What?

ANASTASIA: When we were left behind to look after Alexei.

TATIANA: We swore we'd never talk about it. You'll upset her. It's finished.

ALEXANDRA: I repeat for the last time I don't want you talking to Maria.

MARIA: What happened in the carriage?

ALEXANDRA: My hands are shaking. I haven't had my medicine today. My nerves are on edge. My heart is beating.

ANASTASIA: Sorry. I didn't mean to …

Silence.

Sorry.

KHARITONOV *enters.*

KHARITONOV: [*quietly to* ALEXANDRA, *unable to keep this secret*] The doctor's injected himself, he's like a drunk. He might have done it on purpose! Do you hear him?

He has four concealed carrots and quickly hands a carrot to MARIA. ALEXANDRA *takes it off her and exits. He secretively hands one each to* TATIANA *and* ANASTASIA *and one to* OLGA

YUROVSKY *enters behind* BOTKIN. YUROVSKY *just pushes the wheelchair, letting it roll in.* YUROVSKY *sits centre at the back of the stage next to* MARIA, *who gets up and moves away.*

BOTKIN: Devil take them all … They think I'm a doctor and can cure everything, and I know absolutely nothing, I've forgotten all I ever knew, I remember nothing, absolutely nothing, Devil take it. If Alexei dies, it'll be my fault. I can't get him the medical help from outside.

YUROVSKY: What is wrong with the boy Alexei? I was a medical orderly in the war, so I know something.

BOTKIN: I was once a doctor but I don't remember anything anymore. Nothing.

YUROVSKY: But why would Alexei die?

BOTKIN: [*lightly, with laughter*] Perhaps I'm not really a man, and am only pretending that I've got arms and legs and a head; perhaps I don't exist at all, and only imagine that I walk, and eat, and sleep. [*Crying*] Oh, if only I didn't exist! Oh, how horrific this place is! How petty the restrictions! And then I remembered my son Yuri. Shot in the Great War and I couldn't get him out of my mind … So, I went and had a shot of morphine … and then another …

MARIA *comes down to* BOTKIN *and soothes him.*

YUROVSKY: If it's just a bruised leg? Why does he lie in bed all day?

BOTKIN: Stop with all these questions.

YUROVSKY: A young malingerer who plays the violin.

BOTKIN: [*almost breaking*] So much noise.

YUROVSKY: [*soothing*] I am sorry if the noise disturbs you but the house has to be fortified even more strongly. [*To* TATIANA *and* ANASTASIA] I had to bring in more guards. Honest workers. Reliable comrades.

ACT THREE

MARIA: [*to* BOTKIN] Hadn't you better lie down, doctor?
BOTKIN: It's alright ... thank you ...
KHARITONOV: [*crossing to the wheelchair*] Speaking's a bit difficult, eh Doctor?! Never mind! Our Siberian shamans say, 'In the poppy's dream, lies the vision of the future'.
BOTKIN: How to stop the boy's screams of pain?

    KHARITONOV *wheels* BOTKIN *out.*

OLGA: We gave morphine to soldiers before it ran out. We had concerts in aid of the sufferers. Music heals people.
TATIANA: Ssh, Olga. My sister's nerves are shot to pieces.
MARIA: Olga remembers the war vividly.
TATIANA: For three years, we were Red Cross nurses and then it all became too much.
YUROVSKY: The war was a catastrophe.
TATIANA: The ward was like a nightmare.
OLGA: Only music drowned out the constant screaming.
YUROVSKY: A war created by Imperialist criminals. This house is so dirty, all of it needs cleaning. We may need to transfer you to a safer place. Like in the war.
OLGA: [*tapping a beat*] The constant sound of tapping crutches.
TATIANA: A soldier I loved gave me a little dog and then I never saw him again.
YUROVSKY: The soldier or the dog?

    TATIANA *stares at him coldly and crosses to* OLGA.

When I was a kid we lived under a butcher's shop. One day a flood came through. The rescuers took us upstairs to an apartment. It had carpets and clocks and lapdogs. Little children in soft nightgowns, drinking a steamy, sweet milky drink. Afterwards I kept thinking why do we live like this when my mother works day and night but we are always starving? Our home stinks, boiling bones, blood. Why is there such a difference between them and us? And from then, I looked at the rich, young and old ... with contempt.

    He begins to hum the can-can, his hands indicating the rise and fall of the skirts.

Dada da-da-dah-da ...

He starts to roll a cigarette.
Nurses in the war, eh?
ANASTASIA: I only ever wanted to be an actress.
> OLGA *echoes* YUROVSKY *humming the can-can.*

YUROVSKY: I would like to see that.
ANASTASIA: Really? Do you have a cigarette?
YUROVSKY: You smoke?
ANASTASIA: Father taught me. I don't like it.
> *She takes the unlit cigarette from* YUROVSKY *and puts it to her lips, sitting beside him.*

But see here, I am smoking like Papa. I'm going to be in films one day.
YUROVSKY: If we survive these hard times, I'd like to see that. Your cheeks are very pink.
ANASTASIA: When Chekhov died, they put his body in a train compartment for the conveyance of oysters. Everyone ate oysters at his funeral.
YUROVSKY: [*playing with her*] Who is Chekhov?
ANASTASIA: The famous playwright! He makes our life possible.
YUROVSKY: Ah, that doctor who depicted the horrors of prisoners, on Godforsaken Sakhalin. Doomed to a windswept freezing hell. Only he remembered them.
ANASTASIA: We want to perform his plays.
YUROVSKY: Why not? Next week!
ANASTASIA: Really?
YUROVSKY: He was brave to undertake that journey. He'll inspire you!
> YUROVSKY *puts his hand on her knee and leans in as if to kiss her. The* GUARD *enters.* YUROVSKY *stands.*

GUARD: [*to the girls*] Outside finished. Now you sit inside. Or no soup tonight.
> YUROVSKY *exchanges a look with the* GUARD *and both exit.*

OLGA: Life passes.
TATIANA: We'll never go to Moscow for the trial … I see that we'll never go …
ANASTASIA: I know we will be saved. We will escape over the wall, run away like wolves.

ACT THREE

OLGA: I can't understand how it is that I am still alive.
ANASTASIA: Don't cry, sisters, don't cry.
TATIANA: Go away. I'm not crying, not crying.
MARIA: If I were married I wouldn't ever cry.
TATIANA: You don't respect yourself, flirting with that guard.
MARIA: I think about love ... But it's all turned out to be a nightmare ...
OLGA: We were in the railway carriage ... the soldier stinking of drink. He said, how about you and me? I started to cry. What are you crying for? He attacked me. He held me down. And I kept screaming. The more I struggled the angrier he got. See, he said, blood, you're no different from the rest. I couldn't stop screaming ...

She stares out.

MARIA: But we'll avenge him. We are one heart.
OLGA: I have forgiven him.

Silence as MARIA, *shaken, struggles with this, aware her sisters are watching her reaction.*

ALEXANDRA walks across the stage from right to left, with a candle, without saying anything.

ANASTASIA: She walks as if we will be rescued.
MARIA: But we won't be. I am so angry.

TATIANA and ANASTASIA form a unit. They sit each on one side of OLGA, as MARIA paces. The overall effect is of judges and MARIA as the condemned trying to plead her case.

TATIANA: Maria, you are so selfish. We are all really angry with you.
MARIA: What about you? Never telling me about Olga. You betrayed me.
ANASTASIA: You've become so secretive. I don't know who you are anymore.
MARIA: I will confess to you this once, and never again. [*Softly*] It's my secret ... I can't be silent. I love ... Ivan.
TATIANA: Stop that, I don't hear you, [*sing-song*] I can't hear you.
MARIA: What am I to do? I saw the sweetness in him and I was sorry for him and all he believed.
TATIANA: [*to* ANASTASIA] Unbelievable! He was our gaoler! Where's the romance?!
MARIA: Then I fell in love with him ...

TATIANA: I'm not listening. I hate you. He was a Bolshevik. They have taken away our lives. Talk any nonsense you like, I shan't hear … [*the can-can*] dada da-da-dah-da …
ANASTASIA: Mother says what you did makes you a traitor.
TATIANA: Oh, stop encouraging her.
MARIA: It's my fate. And he loves me.
TATIANA: [*hands to her ears*] Shut up.
MARIA: I am in love with a revolutionary, that means that is my destiny … because nothing is how it was.
TATIANA: Oh, really! Did he put his hands under your dress?
MARIA: You're jealous because no-one loves you.

    TATIANA, *outraged by her statement, covers* OLGA's *ears.*

TATIANA: All Olga's suitors wanted to marry me. Remember?! [*To* ANASTASIA: *Am I wrong? Am I making this up?*] The embarrassment. He wants Tatiana, not Olga. Oh, it's a grand ball and he's on his knees to Tatiana.
MARIA: He was as good as all of them.
TATIANA: [*uncovering* OLGA's *ears*] And you let him kiss you!
MARIA: In the fairytale, Ivan finds the firebird and marries the princess.
ANASTASIA: He wasn't out of a book.
TATIANA: [*wounding her*] He wasn't even good-looking.
MARIA: How can you be so mean?
TATIANA: How could you sink so low?
MARIA: He touched my hand.
TATIANA: And then what?
ANASTASIA: No! That wall outside will never be destroyed! You want to be like them!

    ANASTASIA *exits.*

MARIA: He held me …
TATIANA: A gaoler with a bayonet and his prisoner loves him! You make me sick! No man would ever be as wonderful as Papa …

    TATIANA *exits.*

MARIA: You can punish me with silence and make out I'm bad … but I love him.

    She looks to OLGA, *the only sister left.*

    Whatever happens to us … [*yelling defiantly*] I love him!

ACT THREE

> KHARITONOV *enters from the kitchen. He crosses out to the guards' entrance, as the two sisters just look at each other. He returns with two buckets of water. He lifts the lid of the packing case at the front of the stage. It is a bath.* MARIA *and* OLGA *exit.*
>
> NICHOLAS *enters and drops his dressing-gown. He then wanders upstage calling* KHARITONOV.

NICHOLAS: Don't be shy! Come on! Help me!

> KHARITONOV *enters with a towel over his shoulder and gently massages* NICHOLAS*'s back as he sits in the bath.*

What does Yurovsky want now? I don't understand.

KHARITONOV: [*softly, almost like a prayer*] Your Majesty. You are Emperor and Autocrat of all the Russias.

NICHOLAS: Stop! Scrub my back harder.

KHARITONOV: Emperor and Autocrat of all the Russias. From the White Sea to the Black Sea, from the Pacific to the Baltic. The guards can't get more water, it takes too much time, it's a nuisance.

NICHOLAS: I need to be clean before prayers.

KHARITONOV: Emperor and Autocrat of all the Russias. From the White Sea to the Black Sea, from the Pacific to the Baltic. They say there'll be no more baths.

NICHOLAS: I need to soak in hot water for my aches and pains. It's so little to ask for.

KHARITONOV: Scratch between the shoulder blades?

NICHOLAS: Ah, it's why I abdicated in the railway carriage. Divine right. I never wanted it. I wasn't angry then, I gave it all away with the swipe of a pen. My wife wept but I slept in peace for the first time. All that matters, Kharitonov, is baths, exercise and good food, weather and the family. Hang it all, I get so tense when I can't have five hot baths a day. Now go away and I'll just soak.

> KHARITONOV *takes three steps backwards, pauses and looks at* NICHOLAS.

KHARITONOV: There's nowhere to go.

NICHOLAS: What has Yurovsky got against my baths? Tell me straight.

KHARITONOV: God bless you, sire. Yurovsky says all water is needed to wash the dishes.

NICHOLAS: But you've just put soap all over my back.

KHARITONOV: He won't give me another bucket.

NICHOLAS: I believed I was doing the right thing by the country. They tore up all the maps so a new map could be created. But there was no map, only cruelty, terror and greed. I am at a loss as to what to do. They have no interest in the Russia I once knew, and which has gone forever. It's why I take my baths. They help me forget I am lost. For this half hour, I know where I am.

KHARITONOV: The priest will be here in the morning. Yurovsky says he can bless us.

NICHOLAS: The soap needs to be washed off.

KHARITONOV: It'll be like oil on your back. That can't be a bad thing.

NICHOLAS: When I married, I thought we would be happy … and that all of us will be saved by God's grace. But now, not even a bucket of hot water. [*Weeping*] My dear, dear Kasha, don't believe me, don't believe me …

> *He gets out of the bath and* KHARITONOV *exits with him.*
>
> *Lighting change.*

END OF ACT THREE

ACT FOUR

Late at night, two days later. The sounds of a heavy artillery barrage getting closer. The violin music from offstage.

The GUARD *enters the empty space and listens, hands clasped as if in prayer, then shouts.*

GUARD: Shut up!

The music stops abruptly.

It's our music now. Not yours!

As the GUARD *exits, she crosses* YUROVSKY's *path.* YUROVSKY *carries the Red banner and stands it against the back wall.* ALEXANDRA *enters. She turns and looks at the banner. Both with their backs to the audience.*

ALEXANDRA: What is that monstrosity?

YUROVSKY looks at her and crosses to sit on the packing case near the guards' exit.

YUROVSKY: Art for the people. Your daughter is interested in art. We have the train at the station. Brightly coloured. We perform plays. She could take part.

ALEXANDRA: What?

YUROVSKY: She sits in a cage. The people will see the last relic of the Tsarist dynasty.

ALEXANDRA: [*turning to him*] Like some freak in your circus?

YUROVSKY: If you join the train we could take you across the country to Moscow. A guarantee of safety.

ALEXANDRA: And be a laughing stock? Anastasia in a cage. All the sickness in me, I give to you. May the sickness bring you agony …

She turns away and exits.

Goodnight.

YUROVSKY crosses into the upper exit where the family rooms are and pulls out KHARITONOV *by the ear, dragging him centre stage, where* KHARITONOV *falls on his knees.* MARIA *watches in the upstage entrance to the kitchen.*

YUROVSKY: You … is this the flour you have been hiding?

KHARITONOV: Yes.

YUROVSKY: Hoarding is a crime, Citizen. Punishable by hanging. Sprinkle the flour. Why are you still wearing those 'whites'?

KHARITONOV: This is my uniform.

YUROVSKY: There are no more uniforms. Take them off.

KHARITONOV *peels off his cook's uniform.*

KHARITONOV: I feel … disembowelled.

YUROVSKY *opens the lid of the bath. Wets his hands.*

YUROVSKY: Now dust your face with flour. [*To* MARIA] Not you. Stand aside. This is a baptism for servants who are counter revolutionaries [*patting* KHARITONOV*'s cheeks with flour*] to turn them into ghosts.

KHARITONOV: Am I no longer a chef?

YUROVSKY: There is the working class and then the communists. That is all that is left in Russia. So, it is good to look like a ghost. We can't kill ghosts.

KHARITONOV: I feel like a vagrant like this.

YUROVSKY: I am satisfied you are compliant. You are free to leave this house.

KHARITONOV: After midnight? Like this?

MARIA: What will happen to him?

YUROVSKY: He will have to find a hole in the road to sleep in.

KHARITONOV: The Empress needs high quality care. I must stay with her.

MARIA: I am afraid for him.

YUROVSKY: Then you will be moved to a safer place.

As KHARITONOV *exits,* BOTKIN *enters with* OLGA *tightly holding the handles of the wheelchair.*

BOTKIN: What's the matter?

YUROVSKY: There is an artillery barrage. The Whites are closing in. It's too unsafe to stay in the upper rooms. You all need to go down to the basement. Tell them to get ready to leave.

BOTKIN: Are we to pack?

ACT FOUR

YUROVSKY: Just get rid of what you don't need. [*Indicating a packing case*] Your cases and goods will follow you later. Now for your immediate safety you must vacate these rooms.

OLGA: We must stay together.

BOTKIN: She never sleeps nights. It's when she is most awake and lucid. When the others are sleeping.

YUROVSKY: Wake the others. There is little time. Change into your travelling clothes. There's a few hours left.

MARIA crosses throughout with blankets and clothes, placing them in a packing case.

BOTKIN: For what?

YUROVSKY: To solve the problems of your safety. We have to move you under the cover of darkness so the townspeople won't lynch you or the workers attack you. The truck has arrived to transport you.

BOTKIN: Where?

YUROVSKY: To a better place.

He sits on the front packing case.

Orders from Moscow.

    ANASTASIA *enters.*

ANASTASIA: What is it?

BOTKIN: We are leaving.

Pause. ANASTASIA *moves down to* YUROVSKY *and sits next to him on the packing case. Her eyes meet his. She drops her eyes as he continues to stare at her.*

ANASTASIA: Will we see you again?

YUROVSKY: Because of your good behaviour you are being moved on. Your sentence has been lessened.

ANASTASIA: You never saw the play.

She looks at him, hands him back the cigarette he gave her.

Will we meet again sometime?

YUROVSKY: In ten years? We'll hardly know each another then; you'll have lived in England as an actress. You'll say, 'How do you do?' with roses in your cheeks. Good luck to you and don't be trouble when you go.

He tears up the cigarette, standing suddenly and moving upstage.
Now hurry.
BOTKIN: There will be chaos out there.
The GUARD *enters upstage.*
GUARD: The town is being bombarded.
KHARITONOV: [*shouting off*] What about food?!
YUROVSKY: Housekeeping will be provided where you are going. There are supplies in the truck. The Empress can write instructions as to what she wants sent on first of all.

YUROVSKY *exits out the guards' door, throwing away the belt that Oxana took off Nicholas.*

KHARITONOV *enters, embarrassed, trying to conceal his lack of uniform.*

BOTKIN: We may never see him again; people like him will be moved around to do their cold-blooded work. Yes ... perhaps this time our life will change and I will be able to retire and get a pension in England. How radical! Life will be so quiet ... so agreeable, respectable ...
ANASTASIA: Yes, dear Doctor, wherever we go we will always look after you.
BOTKIN: [*singing softly*] Tar-ara-boom-de-ay ...

BOTKIN *suddenly notices* KHARITONOV.

KHARITONOV: It feels as if all the ingredients were mixed up, meat with icing, cherries with cabbage. Still, with all my soul I wish us happiness wherever we go.
BOTKIN: Where are your whites? What happened to your face?
KHARITONOV: Better to be safe than sorry.
BOTKIN: What are you wearing? A tea towel?
KHARITONOV: What about it?
BOTKIN. I could tell you what you look like now, but it wouldn't be polite.
KHARITONOV: A chef's whites stink of former people. Nobody likes it, but it's all one to me. I'm glad to be with you. Whether I've got a chef's hat or not, I'm happy to be with you.
ANASTASIA: Let's see if you can have some of father's clothes.

ANASTASIA *exits with* KHARITONOV.

ACT FOUR

BOTKIN: [*singing*] It is my washing day ...
    Tar-ara-boom-de-ay ...

    OLGA *wheels* BOTKIN *to the front as* MARIA *approaches closer.*

    Mayhem as packing takes place, increasingly chaotic all around.

MARIA: Are you ready?

BOTKIN: What for?

MARIA: [*sitting, her back half turned to him*] Nothing. Do you love my mother, and father, and all of us?

BOTKIN: Very much.

MARIA: Who loves you the most?

BOTKIN: I don't remember that.

MARIA: When Rasputin used to visit us at night in the dark, he'd say, 'Light is shining from me from my fingers; all my light is here for you'.

BOTKIN: Was it?

MARIA: Now I can't even see the sky. There's Papa ... all my hopes for him have gone. He has no power to change anything.

    NICHOLAS *enters agitated. He picks up the belt Yurovsky tossed away.*

NICHOLAS: When are we going to leave this house? The waiting is awful. [*He looks at his watch.*] Yurovsky gave me back my belt. My watch. One o'clock in the morning precisely.

    Pause.

BOTKIN: We are to file down the staircase in a precise order. They will escort us.

NICHOLAS: Are they also abandoning this house? Something happened yesterday for them to change their plans.

BOTKIN: I don't know ... it's all one ... we will be gone.

    NICHOLAS *is behind* MARIA *as she sits.*

NICHOLAS: It is as if these Reds want to suffocate me. To stop me breathing in the sun and feeling the wind from the steppes, that smell of earth and wild grass.

MARIA: And Ivan?

BOTKIN: What about Ivan?

MARIA: Our soldiers may wound Ivan.
BOTKIN: [*terse*] Maria, you are young and pretty, there will be other men. One Bolshevik more or less—what difference does it make?
GUARD: [*shouting*] Hurry up!
   An increasing sense of urgency.
NICHOLAS: Even though Yurovsky is a vile specimen. One must be compliant. I mean it's our best hope of survival until we are rescued.
MARIA: [*getting up, upset*] I won't leave this house, Ivan won't know where to find me …
NICHOLAS: [*trying to reason with her*] These rooms will be empty.
MARIA: Tell Yurovsky. I have nothing to take. Nothing. Just the touch of Ivan's hand in mine.
NICHOLAS: [*frustrated*] I feel utterly helpless.
BOTKIN: [*with urgency*] Perhaps they'll separate us and we'll never meet again, so here's my advice. Put on your hat, take a stick in your hand, go. Go on and on, without looking round. And the farther you go, away from Russia, the better.
GUARD: [*going up to* BOTKIN] What are you complaining about, old man?
BOTKIN: Stop it!
OLGA: [*to* MARIA] Our friend sat with me. He offered me an orange half peeled. I could smell dead bodies. The sweetness of them was sickening. Ivan's too.
MARIA: I don't believe you.
OLGA: Ivan wasn't shipped off to the front. They're lying.
MARIA: Stop!
OLGA: He didn't die from typhus.
MARIA: No. Please don't.
OLGA: But still our friend wanted me to share the orange. It was all he had.
BOTKIN: I don't know. It's all nonsense.

   OLGA *wheels* BOTKIN *in a circle to the upstage area.*

   KHARITONOV *comes in as the* GUARD *exits.* KHARITONOV *is now dressed like* NICHOLAS.

KHARITONOV: Will we take the Dynasty of the Romanovs book with us?
NICHOLAS: Go away! Leave me! Please!

ACT FOUR

KHARITONOV: Emperor, this book is about the great love we have for you and your ancestors.
NICHOLAS: Oh, what has become of my past and where is it? What do you want? [*Seeing the irony of the cook in his clothes*] Emperor!
KHARITONOV: What? The book.
NICHOLAS: Emperor. I'm tired of you.

    KHARITONOV *hands* NICHOLAS *the book, which he doesn't take.*

KHARITONOV: It will be winter soon.
NICHOLAS: Better snow than these mosquitoes driving us mad. They care not for Emperors either. Proletarians the lot of them. I want to go back to the past. Those leisurely days with wifey and my children happy with goose baked with cabbage, after-dinner naps … In England, we will have fun … And now you are in my clothes!
KHARITONOV: [*upset*] I apologise. I never intended to—
NICHOLAS: [*interrupting him*] What a terrible way to show my gratitude to you. You who have been my friend … Now you are dressed for death. My dear girls, my boy, my beautiful daughters! My wife …

    ALEXANDRA *enters with a violin case which she holds close to her.*

ALEXANDRA: You'll disturb Alexei. Are you sure it's not a false alarm? Where are we going in the middle of the night? Nothing is packed. My legs are hurting. I ache all over. It's so inconsiderate. Why can't they wait till morning?

    TATIANA *and* ANASTASIA *enter now, putting on the sashes they made earlier.*

NICHOLAS: [*confused*] I'm speaking quietly. Besides we have to do what they ask of us.
ALEXANDRA: Alexei can't walk.
NICHOLAS: [*looking through the book*] Alright. I'll carry him. Leave the book, Kharitonov. After all it doesn't belong to us but the previous owner of this house.
ALEXANDRA: Can't you reason with Yurovsky, so we can stay a little longer? Or is he afraid our armies will strike theirs down?
TATIANA: Have we all put on the sashes? You Mama? Put a sash on Olga.
ANASTASIA: Why doesn't Maria have a jewelled sash on?

TATIANA: [*undertone*] Can't trust her!

    ANASTASIA *takes a sash for* OLGA *and wraps it around her.*

ANASTASIA: For where we go next. Security. To help us live.

OLGA: The guns are booming. Remember our friend and his love. I can't remember his voice. His voice has gone.

    The sound of distant explosions.

    YUROVSKY *enters and crosses down to the front as he looks at them.*

YUROVSKY Everything comes to an end. You are being sent to London.

    KHARITONOV *drops the Romanov book in shock.* NICHOLAS *and* ALEXANDRA *stand up from the packing case in the centre at the back.* BOTKIN, ANASTASIA, MARIA *and* OLGA *cluster upstage.*

TATIANA: We don't want to leave Russia, but it seems we are being made to, all the same.

YUROVSKY: If anything happens, ask the next Committee to contact me.

TATIANA: This means there's no chance of a trial in Moscow.

YUROVSKY: We want the best for your family. I, the son of a worker, have the great task of seeing the Imperial family on their way out of here. [*To* MARIA] You! You don't want to die here. I hear you don't want to go.

MARIA: [*stepping towards him*] I want to wait for Ivan.

ANASTASIA: Don't, don't.

    MARIA *is crying bitterly.* YUROVSKY *puts his arm around her shoulder and takes her to one side.*

YUROVSKY: [*quietly*] Ivan was shipped off to the front where he was wounded, fell sick with typhus. He is dead. I don't want you to torment yourself with thoughts he might be alive and waiting for you. Take her, Tatiana … it's time … down to the basement for a final photograph.

TATIANA: If you come with us, we'll forgive you.

GUARD: To the basement! The basement!

    He goes out quickly. NICHOLAS *is uncertain how to comfort* MARIA.

MARIA: I'm going out of my mind … the locket was to protect him.

ACT FOUR

TATIANA: Don't, Maria, don't … he would have had a horrible life if they had found it on him.
MARIA: I'm not crying any more. Did Oxana keep the locket? Was it because I gave the magic away I couldn't save him?
YUROVSKY: To the basement!
TATIANA: We have to leave. Just remember how he kissed you.
MARIA: [*angrily*] I never want to come back here. I really hate it.

>ALEXANDRA *kisses* NICHOLAS *and leans against him, clinging to him.*

ALEXANDRA: I can hardly move, my back aches. They'll have to carry me out of here. Remember, Nicky, how we thought we'd never marry? Everyone was against it. But no power could break us apart and you are always the first person I kiss in the morning and the last I kiss at night, dearest darling.

>*They all listen as a truck drives up.*

TATIANA: They've come for us. Maybe we will be happy now.
ANASTASIA: I hate this house … but now I'm afraid to leave this room. It's where I've kept daydreams alive … But what if imagination is left forever in this room? I had a dream last night.

>BOTKIN, ALEXANDRA, ANASTASIA, NICHOLAS *along with* OLGA, TATIANA, KHARITONOV *and* MARIA *all move to the photographic pose of the beginning as if they are part of this nightmare.*

I'm in a play. But I didn't have my costume and I forgot my lines. I am pelted with eggs and left alone in the theatre. They lock the doors and the lights are turned off. And everything is cold and dark. It felt so real. I was so afraid.

>ALEXANDRA *and* NICHOLAS *stand centre.* ALEXANDRA *holds the violin case in her arms like a small coffin, symbolic of the sleeping Alexei.* OLGA, TATIANA *and* ANASTASIA *stand together,* MARIA *separately.* BOTKIN *in his wheelchair,* KHARITONOV *standing behind the family as if in a portrait.*

>YUROVSKY *stands on the packing case at the back, as if he is a ringmaster.*

YUROVSKY: [*joyous*] A final photograph!
BOTKIN: [*singing*] Tar-ara-boom-de-ay …

NICHOLAS *turns to* BOTKIN *and smiles. He turns back and there is a flash of light and smoke as if a photo has been taken as at the play's beginning.*

A soundscape of guns, repeatedly firing, over and over.

The family hold their photographic pose bathed in red light. They remain frozen in their pose with the Bolsheviks behind them.

In the darkness, MARIA *steps away.*

Lighting/sound change.

MARIA: My broken body in the forest.
Where there are no fences,
No guns, no guards. Only you with me.
Do not close my eyes.
I want to stare up through the trees at the sky.

Blackout.

THE END

presents

TCHEKOV AT THE HOUSE OF SPECIAL PURPOSE

by
R. Johns

28 August – 8 September 2019

MARIA **Joanna Halliday**
ANASTASIA **Natalia Rozpara**
TATIANA **Kandice Joy**
OLGA **Meg McKibbin**
ALEXANDRA **Anita Torrance**
'CITIZEN' NICHOLAS **Jim Daly**
DR EUGENY BOTKIN **Phil Roberts**
KHARITONOV **Gregory J. Fryer**
OXANA **Olga Makeeva**
GUARD **Maria Paula Afanador**
YUROVSKY **Adam May**
IVAN **Huw Jennings**

Director **Alex Menglet**
Production designer **Peter Mumford**
Lighting designer **Shane Grant**
Sound designer and composer **Zac Kazepis**
Costume designer **Michael Mumford**
Stage manager **Julian Adams**

This script and production are dedicated to the original Dr Botkin,
Peter Stratford.

CEO & Artistic Director
Liz Jones

CEO and Manager / Producer
Caitlin Dullard

Venue Manager
Hayley Fox

Front-of-House Manager
Amber Hart

Marketing and Communications
Sophia Constantine

Social Media
Solange Parraguez

Rebuild La Mama Fundraising Manager
Tim Stitz

Learning Producer and School Publications Coordinator
Maureen Hartley

Preservation Coordinator
Fiona Wiseman

Office Co-ordinator
Elena Larkin

Artistic Program Manager
Xanthe Beesley

Curators
Gemma Horbury (Musica); **Amanda Anastasi** (Poetica)

La Mama office is currently at:
La Mama Courthouse, 349 Drummond Street, Carlton, Vic 3053
www.lamama.com.au | info@lamama.com.au
facebook.com/lamama.theatre | twitter.com/lamamatheatre
Office phone 03 9347 6948 | Office Mon–Fri, 10:30am–5:30pm

FRONT OF HOUSE STAFF

Alex Woollatt, Amber Hart, Anna Ellis, Caitlin Dullard, Carmelina Di Guglielmo, Darren Vizer, Dennis Coard, Isabel Knight, Laurence Strangio, Maureen Hartley, Robyn Clancy, Sophia Constantine, Susan Bamford-Caleo, Dora Abraham, Elena Larkin, Solange Parraguez and Zac Kazepis.

COMMITTEE OF MANAGEMENT

Richard Watts, Dur-é Dara, Ben Grant, Caitlin Dullard, Caroline Lee, David Levin, Helen Hopkins, Sue Broadway, Beng Oh and Liz Jones.

We are grateful to all our philanthropic partners and donors, advocates, volunteers, audiences, artists and our entire community as we work towards the La Mama rebuild. Thank you!

La Mama Theatre is on traditional land of the Kulin Nation. We give our respect to the Elders of these traditional lands and to all Aboriginal and Torres Strait Islander people past, present and future. We acknowledge all events take place on stolen lands and that sovereignty was never ceded.

La Mama is financially assisted by the Australian Government through the Australia Council—its arts funding and advisory body, the Victorian Government through Creative Victoria—Department of Premier and Cabinet, and the City of Melbourne through the Arts and Culture triennial funding program.

ACKNOWLEDGEMENTS

The inspiration for this work came when I visited St Petersburg with my sister, Jennifer, who encouraged our many adventures that fired up my imagination.

Anton Chekhov for inspiring me with his classic text *Three Sisters*. Chekhov is a genius and his work has been an influence throughout my life in theatre.

The readers of the first drafts, Olga Makeeva and later Peter Stratford. I will always remember Peter reading the entire play to me, with a different voice for each of the twelve characters.

My partner Peter Mumford for his initial brilliant design ideas and ways to make the play live. His endless moral support and creative suggestions. Peter has created the arresting design for the book, in homage to artist Lazar Markovich Lissitzky. *Beat the Whites with the Red Wedge* is a lithographic Soviet propaganda poster. The house is the Ipatiev house in Ekaterinburg where the Romanovs were imprisoned.

Lazlo Suba and his dramaturg Ágota Breczki in Hungary for the early development of the script. Lazlo came briefly to Melbourne to visit family, and auditions and a workshop were held with Laszlo, Miklos Gerely and myself. However, ultimately economic imperatives prevented Lazlo from returning to Australia from Hungary.

Director Alex Menglet, firstly for his contribution to the script. He immediately told me the first Bolshevik commissar needed to be a woman, due to the role women played in the Revolution. He disliked some of the language in the first act and insisted I needed to think how difficult it might be for the Bolsheviks to deal with the Tsar family. That, despite abdication and revolution, the glamour and remoteness of royalty would have affected the way guards spoke or treated the Romanovs. Secondly his aesthetic throughout the process was 'Cut, cut, cut! Simpler! Simpler!' Thirdly his spontaneous, beautiful and fearless direction.

To the wonderful cast and creatives for their thoughts and offers— what a joyous time we had together in the formation of the production.

To John Lloyd Fillingham for his generosity, perception and flair in producing a beautiful and compelling rehearsal video, Jeremy Press for being our wonderful video archivist and perching at impossible angles to capture the work, and Adrian Prosen as my lifesaver for matters technical at MDM, always helping me meet deadlines with a smile.

The production was first supported by La Mama in 2017 in the Centenary of the Russian Revolution. My thanks to Liz Jones, artistic director and CEO of La Mama, and to Caitlin Dullard, CEO, manager and producer, for programming this play at La Mama Courthouse— both are fellow lovers of Chekhov. Thanks too to La Mama for selecting it to be submitted to the VCAA for consideration for their Playlist. I truly appreciate Liz's support of my work over many years and giving me opportunities to develop my voice and craft as a female playwright. Thanks too, to Maureen Hartley, for her support, editing, friendship and guidance as La Mama's Learning Producer.

To the VCAA for programming this work on the 2019 VCE Theatre Studies Playlist. And thanks to all the wonderful La Mama family at Drummond St Courthouse.

Finally, our collective of theatre practitioners would like to acknowledge the traditional lands of the Kulin Nation and pay our respects to elders past, present, and future on whose land this production has been rehearsed and presented.

Left to right: Alseen Mauthoor, Jim Daly, Meg Spencer, Alice Batt (hidden) and Yvette Turner in the 2017 production of TCHEKOV AT THE HOUSE OF SPECIAL PURPOSE *at La Mama Courthouse. Photo: Laura Owsianka.*

WRITER'S NOTE

I was inspired to begin this project in St Petersburg when I was on my way to Stockholm for the International Women Playwrights' Conference which was presenting my work. One summer evening I found the Hermitage Museum (and the site of the Winter Palace and Revolution) was open. In the near empty building, I was sitting on a window ledge staring down at the Neva River and the idea floated into my mind that I had to write about the four young Romanov sisters, who, with the once Tsar and Tsarina, were imprisoned in 1917-18. In my research, I discovered that the girls performed the short plays of Chekhov during their imprisonment. It seemed an appropriate time in our twenty-first century to tell those women's stories–'her-stories', at a time when civil wars were erupting and revolutionary philosophies were taking hold, now, as well as then.

I thus deconstructed Chekhov's *Three Sisters*, as a way of seeing into the lives of the Romanov sisters, setting the story seventeen years on from 1901 when it was first produced, to the time of the Russian Revolution; to the time of the final encounter between the Romanov family and the Bolsheviks. My play *Tchekov at the House of Special Purpose* became a themed narrative set in a claustrophobic room full of travelling cases with a family seemingly in transit.

Note: the spelling of Chekhov in the title as 'Tchekov' references the teasing of Anastasia, the youngest Romanov daughter, by one of the Bolsheviks. The last house of the Romanovs' imprisonment was actually named by the Bolsheviks in 1918, The House of Special Purpose.

The work raises questions about love, belief and family in times of war and chaos, and asks what makes us human in times of profound political, social and existential crisis.

In Chekhov's *Three Sisters* the Prozorov family dream of getting to Moscow and escaping their stifling lives in a provincial town. The sisters' guests are army officers, love affairs develop, there is a death by gunshot and their lives move on to an unknown future. The family in the *Three Sisters* were said to live in Perm. The next stop on that railway line was Ekaterinburg, where the exiled Citizen Nicholas and his family were later imprisoned.

How many of us know the strangely synchronistic story from Russian history of the Tsar (who has abdicated) and his family, also trapped in a provincial town. They wait to get to Moscow to be tried by Trotsky, and are surrounded by the Bolshevik guards in a house where they hope for rescue or liberation. It is known that the daughters of the Tsar performed *The Bear* by Chekhov during their imprisonment at Tobolsk.

In this production, disturbance is the starting point, as the soldiers in this provincial house are not guests, as in *Three Sisters*, but guards. Guards who are possibly as confused about the end point of their surveillance as the now-named 'Citizen' Nicholas, his family and retainers are about their imprisonment. Tension and denial build until this family and their retainers are bundled into the basement, where they sit and wait, not knowing their fate. Thus the end of a world order and the birth of a new order are played out in the suffocating rooms in a provincial house during summer. Yet again, like Chekhov's family, this family also dream, have ambitions, fall in love and hold onto a belief that life may still change for the better.

DIRECTOR'S NOTE

Realistic likeness to historical characters is the province of books, films, museums and the internet. Rather, what this drama intends to do is 'vibrate', to awaken interest, 'inject psyches' with how we stay human when life takes us to challenging places.

The duty of the director is paramount in rehearsal; the director has to 'infect' the actors with the theme of the play, so that all are stylistically in the same play and 'on the same page'.

My aim for this production is to inspire, not 'teaching' history, but to excite the actors and audience alike about the process. We want to give the audience history, cooked a different way. It's not didactic, cold blooded history as a slice of life, rather a chance for the audience to hear the human heartbeat behind the story through the performances. The twelve actors are creating a modern contemporary vibration of the Australian heart looking at that period. Actors are living history; they are not historical truth. The aim of the actor is to bring time to life, so living, breathing Russian history spills into Australia today. To help the audience 'breathe', by reminding them what they do not want to become.

My aim is for twelve Australian actors to tell a Russian story as seen through twenty-first century Australian eyes, exploring the resonances of that story and what it means to us. It is a way of seeing the world through our sensibility. We live in a twenty-first century of dislocated peoples, which is also the theme of this play. It is an ode to life and love, the desire for freedom as a way to resist brutality.

LANGUAGE

The playwright draws on Chekhov's writing style and use of language to tell some of the story.

Doctor Botkin is the most Chekhovian character—this is because Chekhov was a doctor and he wrote the doctor into many of his plays—so in this production the Doctor comments on the old order and the fears associated with the new order. He represents what was humane, secure and stable opposite the anarchy of revolution.

The Bolsheviks, particularly the Guard, are more, brutal, down-to-earth, basic, and have less fluidity with language. However, the naïve young Guard Ivan has visions of utopia, while dealing with the practical realities of establishing it. His language at times is more heightened.

Citizen Nicolas and Tsarina are from a world already gone, but they hang onto remnants of their language to make their life understandable in this chaotic situation. With an attitude that everyone is still a servant who should obey her, the Tsarina's language demonstrates a disconnection from the reality of the situation she faces.

The boy Tsarevitch is always offstage, his 'voice' defined by violin playing, as if he is a learner, symbolically practising for an impossible future.

Left to right: Meg Spencer, Adam May, Peter Stratford and Yvette Turner in the 2017 production of TCHEKOV AT THE HOUSE OF SPECIAL PURPOSE at La Mama Courthouse. Photo: Laura Owsianka

USE OF SPACE, DESIGN ELEMENTS AND PROPS

The production design in this project is geared to showing the decline of the old order and the rise of the new reality that faces the Tsarist Romanovs in a time of revolution.

The La Mama Courthouse venue is perfect for the regional provincial house that was designated as the last place of imprisonment for the once Tsar and his family. The venue has been specially chosen for its architectural qualities and period features.

The whole room/stage is used for the set, the doorways featured and exposed. Within the room there is an installation of the family's belongings packed into suitcases, travelling trunks and tea chests, from which props can be withdrawn. However, while the stage area is exposed, black curtains are used to enclose the audience seating bank. This encourages the audience to see themselves as voyeurs observing what is happening on the stage as they observe the decline of the family's fortunes.

Tea chests are piled high at the back of the set, enabling a secret walkway for actors. The arrangement of trunks is designed to transition into seats and tables in performance. And even into a bath for Citizen Nicholas.

A vintage wheelchair is used for the Doctor, symbolizing the sickness and feebleness of the old regime. The heaviness of the chair, and the difficulty for the actors in manoeuvring it, are symbolic of loss of power.

LIGHTING

Lighting and haze are used in the production to suggest a photographic camera. At the end of the play, this device is used as a metaphor for the family execution.

There is a very small chandelier which is used to add atmosphere to the room. Its size is symbolic of the loss of grandeur and sumptuousness of the Romanovs' past.

AUDIO VISUAL

The AV component is a non-naturalistic, Absurdist intrusion in the play, referencing Hollywood silent movies, with captions in Russian and English.

SOUND

The soundscape features contemporary music *Mutter* (Mother) by Rammstein (German industrial metal band) to which the sisters, Nicholas and (the German born) Tsarina Alexandra dance a minuet. The mosquito sounds are both naturalistic and symbolic of danger, as a mosquito is a parasite that sucks blood. The summer swarms of mosquitoes create a growing sense of unease.

COSTUMES AND SYMBOLISM

Costumes are constructed from contemporary clothing and material that has been refashioned into period attire.

Colour is used symbolically–red versus white. The Reds, once the dispossessed, are now the powerful. The Whites, once absolute rulers, are now the powerless. The daughters are all dressed in white, symbolizing the colour once used by the ruling family. The long johns of Citizen Nicholas are also light coloured.

The Bolsheviks are dressed in red jodhpurs with black leather boots and black leather jackets according to status. Guard Ivan wears heavy style World War I army boots, giving him the gait of a horse.

APPROACH TO PERFORMANCE STYLE

There are elements of Brecht in the production. Brecht takes big topics and reduces them to the experiences of a few people. This is the Russian Revolution played out in one room of a provincial house.

One of the fundamental objectives of Brecht was social change, so the emphasis must not be on individual characters, but their interaction with the rest of the cast within the greater story. This is very evident with this cast of twelve, as focus and emphasis constantly changes.

The power and potential menace inherent in the new status of the Bolsheviks is expressed through the actors' body language and physicality.

Director Alex Menglet merges the language of the modern European and Australian theatre with the Chekhovian tradition, the analytical with the emotional and the absurd. Actors move from a naturalism to stylized physicality and non-naturalism, as in the silent movie sequence, generated by Anastasia, and with the dancing of the Minuet and the Waltz.

Theatre of the Absurd is also present in the food the Romanovs seldom eat, the Chekhov play they never perform and in the game of charades that upturns the old order with Nicholas as a horse and Oxana, the Commissar, as a rider on his back.

ROSEMARY JOHNS
PLAYWRIGHT

Rosemary studied at Manchester University, Tulane and U.C.R. Rosemary received a DFAT grant, Australia now Germany, 2017. The Staatstheater Nürnberg played Black Box 149 (original production La Mama, VCE Playlist) in repertoire–the first time this German state company has curated an Australian work. Her work has been presented in Mumbai, Athens, Stockholm, Cape Town and Christchurch. With the La Mama Learning Program, she has had five works selected for the VCE playlists. Production highlights include co–directing with Peter Stratford Carrying Shoes into the Unknown (La Mama, VCE Playlist) and At the Centre of Light (La Mama/12th Night Theatre Brisbane). Rosemary was AWGIE nominated for Youth and Community Theatre with As Told By The Boys Who Fed Me Apples. (Big West Festival, La Mama)

ALEX MENGLET
DIRECTOR

Alex comes from an established Russian theatrical family. He was trained at the Academy of Performing Arts in Moscow. In Australia, Alex has worked for the MTC, STC, QTC, Playbox/Malthouse, Belvoir St Theatre, Bell Shakespeare Company, Anthill, the State Theatre of South Australia, 45 Downstairs and Red Stitch. Film and television work includes He Died with a Falafel in his Hand, Children of the Revolution, Salvation, The Petrov Affair, Wentworth and Kath and Kim. Alex has directed Playing the Victim, Yellow Moon, Jack Goes Boating and The Rites of Evil (all at Red Stitch), Crime and Punishment (for Alliance Française) and Tchekov at the House of Special Purpose (at La Mama). Alex is a Green Room Award winner and a Helpmann Awards nominee.

PETER MUMFORD
PRODUCTION DESIGNER

Peter has designed for dance, drama and opera companies across Australia. He was a founding member of The Torch Projects and resident designer with Red Stitch Actors Theatre 2005-2013. He gained a Best Production Green Room Award for *Harvest*, and a Green Room Award nomination for *Red Sky Morning*. In 2014 he received the Green Room Award for Best Design for *Foxfinder*. He designed Rodney Hall's early opera projects for Woodend Winter Arts Festivals, and the premiere of Rodney Hall and Paul Dean's new opera *Dry River Run* 2018, Queensland Conservatorium of Music. For Rosemary Johns, he has designed many plays, including *Stray* and *As Told By The Boys Who Fed Me Apples*, both produced at Big West Festival and La Mama.

SHANE GRANT
LIGHTING DESIGNER

Shane has worked extensively with companies including Ranters Theatre, The Torch Project, NYID and many others. He has a BA Dramatic Arts (Production) from VCA. He is currently an artistic director of Metanoia Theatre. He is also a writer and theatre-maker. Recent works are an adaptation of Georges Arnaud's novel *The Wages of Fear* and *Hard-Boiled Bush Noir*. He has written and performed monologues at Gasworks, La Mama and the Mechanics Institute Brunswick. He is currently the Venues Manager at St Martins Youth Arts Centre. He continues to write and light in venues around Melbourne.

ZAC KAZEPIS
SOUND DESIGNER

As a composer and sound designer, Zac has worked on productions including *No One Likes Me* by Darren Vizer and *Three Short Works* by Lloyd Jones at La Mama. He has also composed music for productions at VCA and Adelaide Feast Festival. Zac was sound designer and composer for *Stigma* (Open Stage Theatre/Melbourne Fringe Festival, and interstate seasons). Recently, Zac worked as a composer and sound designer on *Just A Boy, Standing In Front of a Girl* (15 Minutes From Anywhere).

MICHAEL MUMFORD
COSTUME DESIGNER

Michael graduated from Whitehouse Institute of Design in 2011. He designed and produced costumes for the opera *Euridice* (Woodend Winter Arts Festival, dir. Rodney Hall). He recently returned from two years in London working for couturier Antonia Pugh Thomas and is working on his own label and couturier business. He designed costumes for the 2017 La Mama production of *Tchekov at the House of Special Purpose*. He is working towards his Masters degree.

JULIAN ADAMS
STAGE MANAGER

Julian graduated from La Trobe's BA, after completing a Diploma of Live Theatre Services with Melbourne Polytechnic. A jack-of-all-trades, Julian is always looking for a new opportunity to challenge his skills. Recent successes include lighting design for *Echoes*, (La Mama, 2017), *Bipolar Bear* (Fringe, 2016), stage management for *Monash in Love and War* (Chapel Off Chapel, 2018), sound design for *Creatures of The Deep* (Fringe 2018, Sustainability Festival 2019) and acting in *The Seagull* (2018, LTU), *ManDogMan* (MonsterFest 2017) and *King Lear* (2017, LTU).

JOANNA HALLIDAY
MARIA

Joanna trained in Music Theatre at Showfit and completed her Bachelor in Acting at VCA, where she played Abigail Williams in *The Crucible* (dir. Adena Jacobs), and Henry in *Henry V* (dir. Leith McPherson). Joanna debuted as Juliet in Melbourne Shakespeare Company's *Romeo and Juliet* and has performed in *Love's Labour's Lost* and *Travesties*. Joanna will appear in the feature film *Ride Like a Girl* (dir. Rachel Griffiths.) Joanna has trained in singing, classical piano, violin and classical and contemporary dance.

NATALIA ROZPARA
ANASTASIA

At the age of thirteen Natalia performed in *The Silver Donkey* (Children's Performing Company of Australia), which toured the US, including to Disneyland and off-off-Broadway). Natalia trained at Verve Studios' Professional Acting Studio and performed in *With You, Alone* (Theatre Works). She studied a Bachelor of Acting for Stage and Screen at Federation University's Arts Academy, where she acted in *Mother Courage and Her Children*. Natalia also trained in physical theatre at Zen Zen Zo and studied at The Film Space. In 2018 she appeared in feature film *Angel of Mine* (dir. Kim Farrant).

KANDICE JOY
TATIANA

Kandice trained at The Second City Improv Hollywood, LA, RADA, UK (The Shakespeare Award), Pineapple Studios, London, and is now at Howard Fine Acting Studio, Australia. Her television and film credits include *Winners & Losers*; *Underbelly*; *Fat Tony & Co*; *Utopia*; hosting *Creative Kids*; *Sammy Kingsford* (US web series); *Predestination*; *Rhyme & Reason*; *Kath & Kimderella*; *Milk & Cookies*;

Aura and *Knock 'Em Dead*. At the age of nine, Kandice played July in the Australian production of *Annie* and appeared in *Candy Man* (Arts Centre Melbourne). In 2017, Kandice represented Australia in Malaysia, (CSTD International Dance Competition) and continues training at The May Downs School of Dance. Kandice is delighted about performing at La Mama.

MEG MCKIBBIN
OLGA

Meg graduated from WAAPA with a Bachelor of Arts (Music Theatre) in 2017. At WAAPA, she appeared as Abigail Williams in *The Crucible*, and Heather Duke in *Heathers: the Musical*. She made her debut as a female understudy in *A Midsummer Night's Dream* (Australian Shakespeare Company) and as a core cast member in *Treasure Hunt!* (Echelon Productions). She performed in the short film *Gaslight* (finalist; St Kilda Film Festival) and *Twelfth Night* (Melbourne Shakespeare Company, 2019.)

ANITA TORRANCE
ALEXANDRA

Anita's career in Australia includes key guest roles on *Blue Heelers* and *Stingers*, as well as performing in theatre, where she had the opportunity to work with directors Rosemary Johns, David Myles and Lucy Freeman. While en-route to Canada, Anita secured the regular role of Tess Adamson in New Zealand's popular television show, *Shortland Street*. In Vancouver, Anita has worked on such shows as *Smallville* and *Caprica*. She has trained as an actor extensively in both Australia and North America. Anita is thrilled to be back at La Mama, performing in *Tchekov at The House of Special Purpose*.

JIM DALY
'CITIZEN' NICHOLAS

Jim has been an actor for almost 65 years, with wide experience across theatre, film and television. His first television work, at the age of ten, was on a South Australian children's show *Southern Stars*. Highlights of his career have been the two television series of *Pirate Islands*, shot in Australia and Fiji, and the last series of *Rake*. National tours of *Cosi*, *Hello, Goodbye and Happy Birthday*, and *Coranderrk* are amongst his fondest stage memories, along with Ray Mooney's powerful play *Everynight Everynight*, in which he played an insane criminal in H Division in Pentridge Prison. He has just completed *The Ghetto Kabaret*. Next year he will complete an eight-year PhD from Monash on performing grotesquely.

PHIL ROBERTS
DR BOTKIN

Phil was born and raised in England, where he was a member of the Cambridge Footlights Society. After a few years teaching in Papua New Guinea, he moved to Australia and was part of the vibrant arts scene in Canberra. In 1999, he arrived in Melbourne in a production touring to La Mama, and he has remained close to them ever since. Over the course of his career, he has appeared in nearly 200 mainstage productions, and has played a wide variety of roles, from Hamlet to a neurotic caterpillar. As actor and director, Phil has appeared across a number of platforms, including film, television and radio, but independent theatre has always been his greatest passion.

GREGORY J. FRYER
KHARITONOV

Greg has performed in Asia and Europe and as a stand-up at the Melbourne International Comedy Festival. He has featured in several award-winning short films including *The Disappearance of Willy Bingham*. Film and TV includes *The Circuit*, *The Sapphires*, *The Coniston Massacre* (documentary), *The Gods of Wheat Street*, *Mad as Hell*, *Dr Blake*, and *Wake in Fright*. Other performance includes the Coranderrk project and a collaboration with the Lloyd Jones ensemble at La Mama, which he considers his second home.

OLGA MAKEEVA
OXANA

Olga trained in the Stanislavsky method at the State Academy of Theatrical Arts, Moscow. In 1986 she joined the Soviet Army Theatre, performing in Moscow and on tour in the USSR. During perestroika she worked at the Odd & Even Theatre, reviving the avant-garde OBERIU movement suppressed by Stalin. At the 1990 Zurich International Theatre Festival she performed in Vladimir Kazakov's *Don Juan*. Olga came to Melbourne in 1999 and performed in *Playing The Victim* and *Fatboy* (Red Stitch, where she is now an ensemble member). La Mama credits include *Thee Oaks* and *A History of Motion Pictures*.

MARIA PAULA AFANADOR
THE GUARD

Maria studied Performing Arts at the Charlot Academy and The National Theater House in her home country, Colombia, graduating in 2012. In Australia, in 2014, she performed with the Spanish Theater Company in *Erotic Alleluia* (Mechanical Theatre). Performances at La Mama include *The Masque of Beauty* (Peter Green) and *Women on the Verge* (reprised at The Butterfly Club and The Italian Institute of Culture). Maria was part of *Tchekov at The House of Special Purpose* in 2017. She is co-founder of The Bridge, a theatre company of native Spanish speakers. She is interested in creating an artistic community, focusing on the impact of immigrants on the arts.

ADAM MAY
YUROVSKY

Adam has acted in a variety of theatre spaces, including La Mama, Theatreworks, Chapel off Chapel, 45 Downstairs, Northcote Town Hall, Gasworks, Victorian Arts Centre, Regal Theatre Perth, the London Palladium, and the Edinburgh Festival. Film and television credits include the Chinese film *Dogfight*, *Sunshine*, *Utopia*, *Ali's Wedding*, *House Husbands*, *Tangle*, *Blue Heelers*, *Saddle Club*, *One Perfect Day* and *The Secret Life of Us*. He was nominated Best Actor at the 15/15 Festival. Adam wrote *Rising Fish Prayer* (Asialink Playwriting Award winner, broadcast on BBC Radio and published by Currency Press).

HUW JENNINGS
IVAN

Huw graduated from the National Theatre Drama School and the RADA Acting Shakespeare course 2016. He was acknowledged for outstanding achievement in VCE theatre, drama and film-making, featuring in the VCAA Top Acts and Top Screen. His graduate performance was as Laurence Moss in *Abigail's Party*. Since graduating he has toured to the Adelaide Fringe Festival, performed in *Measure For Measure* and *The Gizmo*, created several short films and appeared in feature films *That's Not Me*, *Miss Fisher and the Crypt of Tears* and *Bernie Brown: The Show*.

STANDING OVATION FOR
AUSTRALIA'S HOME OF INDEPENDENT THEATRE

In 2019 La Mama will celebrate 52 years of nurturing new Australian theatre.

Built in 1883 for Anthony Reuben Ford, a Carlton printer, the building in Faraday Street had been used as a workshop, a boot and shoe factory, an electrical engineering workshop and a silk underwear factory before becoming a theatre in 1967. It was established by Betty Burstall and modelled on experimental theatre activities in New York. Jack Hibberd's play *Three Old Friends* was the first play performed in the tiny space. Since that time the crowded intimacy of La Mama has provided welcome opportunities to a host of playwrights, actors, directors, technicians, filmmakers, poets and comedians, such as David Williamson, Barry Dickins, John Romeril, Tes Lyssiotis, Lloyd Jones, the Cantrills, Judith Lucy, Richard Frankland, Julia Zemiro, and Cate Blanchett... the list of those who have been nurtured there is long.

Under the capable care of Liz Jones (Artistic Director and CEO), Caitlin Dullard (Manager/Producer and Co-CEO), and a committed La Mama team, more than 50 productions are produced annually at La Mama, and at a second performance venue, the refurbished La Mama Courthouse, 349 Drummond Street, which was short-listed in May for a 2018 Victorian Australian Institute of Architects Chapter Award. An ever-increasing audience is drawn not only from the Carlton and Melbourne University environs, but from far and wide across the country.

> 'I set La Mama up, as a space for writers and directors to perform in but also it was a space where people came, as audience, to participate in the creative experiment.'
>
> —Betty Burstall, Artistic Director of La Mama 1967–76

La Mama Theatre—which on various occasions has been called headquarters, the shopfront and the birthplace of Australian Theatre—was classified by the National Trust in 1999.

> 'The two-storey brick building is of State cultural significance because it has been occupied by La Mama Theatre... The building is indelibly associated with the performance arts and is a rare manifestation of an experimental theatre in Australia...'
>
> —National Trust Classification Report

Unfortunately in May 2018 La Mama Theatre was extensively damaged by fire, caused by an electrical fault. A huge outpouring of love and support from the Carlton community, from many arts and non-arts organisations, from funding bodies, audience members, media, schools and La Mama's extensive community of artists is helping La Mama to move forward with optimism and energy.

Taking one step at a time, La Mama will continue; planning has begun and the future is bright:

> 'While there is considerable damage, this has become a restoration project. We will retain as much of the historic structure of the building as possible.
>
> We loved our building on Faraday Street, but La Mama is more than a building, and despite our devastation her spirit is strong. Together with our artists, staff and community we will move with strength into the next 50 years and beyond.'
>
> —Liz Jones and Caitlin Dullard

For updates on how you can help La Mama move on, and details of all productions and events visit: www.lamama.com.au

www.ingramcontent.com/pod-product-compliance
Lightning Source LLC
Chambersburg PA
CBHW050020090426
42734CB00021B/3344